LESLIE LINSLEY'S
DÉCOUPAGE

BULFINCH PRESS

NEW YORK · BOSTON

LESLIE LINSLEY'S

DÉCOUPAGE

DESIGN · CREATE · DISPLAY

Principal photography by Jon Aron

PHOTO CREDITS

All photographs by Jon Aron except for the following:
Jeffrey Allen: vi top row middle and middle row left, vii
bottom, viii–1, 30, 31, 35, 53 bottom, 64, 71, 76, 88, 90, 91, 92-3,
95, 96, 150, 151, 152, 169; Courtesy Patina, Key West: 12, 13.

Bulfinch Press

Time Warner Book Group
1271 Avenue of the Americas
New York, NY 10020
Visit our Web site at www.bulfinchpress.com

First Edition

Hardcover ISBN 0-8212-2870-6
(Special Sales Edition ISBN 0-8212-6176-2)

Library of Congress Control Number 2003109612

Designed by Joel Avirom and Jason Snyder
Design assistant: Meghan Day Healey

PRINTED IN CHINA

For my mother,
who taught me découpage,
and my grandfather,
who encouraged creativity

CONTENTS

1 INTRODUCTION

My mother taught me how to do découpage when I was in college, and I sold the first pieces I made. Découpage was never a hobby for me but rather a means to an end while I was looking for a "real" job. My grandfather, a retired architect, made charming wooden boxes with hinges and clasps for us to découpage. The boxes were wonderful before I did a thing to them. It was on these handmade boxes that I first applied my designs, which presented an exquisite introduction to the craft.

When I first started selling my découpage boxes (in the beginning, that was all I made), I was fortunate to meet many celebrities who purchased them. I was selling my work through Henri Bendel, an upscale boutique department store in New York City known for its innovative products. The then-president of Bendel's, Geraldine Stutz, had created a store that had individual boutiques within it. Her approach was to showcase new designers in such areas as costume jewelry, home accessories, gifts, and clothing. Many of today's best-known designers got their start at Bendel's.

LEFT
These little trinket boxes were one of my signature pieces at Henri Bendel. They have become favorite gifts for bridesmaids. I use my tiniest floral cutouts on them.

OPPOSITE
Velvet-lined treasure chest boxes such as this one were originally commissioned by the famed New York jewelry store Tiffany for displaying jewelry in its Fifth Avenue windows.

One day I was in the store delivering an order when I had the good fortune to meet Steve McQueen and his wife. This bigger-than-life star took to my boxes and later introduced me to his friend Polly Bergen. Over the years they commissioned special-order boxes to give as gifts. Many others, including Jacqueline Onassis, ordered my boxes. These boxes were charming and unusual and enabled me to offer something uniquely my own.

The experience at Bendel's led me to Bergdorf Goodman across the street, and then to Tiffany and Cartier, all in the same neighborhood. I now look back on those years as quite special; there was an explosion of creativity, and I was free to design what I think of as my best work. I had a ready-made outlet and an abundance of buyers looking for original products, and they gobbled up my boxes as fast as I could make them.

During this time I was introduced to the famed window designer for Tiffany, Gene Moore. For a brief period he commissioned me to make a series of boxes exclusively for Tiffany. Each half-round box resembled a treasure chest, which would hold a single diamond bracelet or ring for the window displays. The outside of the box was always painted white. Once I had applied twenty coats of varnish over the découpage, the box looked as if it were made of ivory. The découpage designs were created with extremely delicate flowers, stems, and buds, and I lined the inside with brilliant pink velvet. One day while walking down Fifth Avenue, I was stopped in my stride. There in every window was one of my treasure boxes, lid propped open to reveal a spectacular piece of diamond jewelry raised on a tiny pedestal inside the velvet-lined box. There was no greater thrill than to have Gene Moore use my boxes in his window displays.

After that I received orders from Cartier. This time Gramp and I created a special lap desk that would be an exclusive. When Cartier put in its first order for sixty lap desks, my grandfather's only comment was "Are you trying to kill me?" In reality, he confessed that this business we had entered into together was keeping him alive. He lived to be ninety-six and continued to make boxes until the day he died, leaving me with a wonderful legacy of boxes that I still work on, though sparingly. I am parsimonious with his boxes, mixing them with manufactured ones that I also découpage. You can imagine my pleasure when someone brings me a box he or she purchased many years ago to show how it has stood the test of time.

On one of my visits to Bendel's, Geri Stutz asked if I would design a découpage kit just for the store. At the time, I was dating a man who had a graphic design firm. I like to tell people that I couldn't afford to pay him to design the kits, so I had to marry him. Eventually we formed a partnership that led to a boutique line of beautifully packaged kits under the name of our newly formed company, "the whole works." We then designed an adorable little kit in a bag for Bergdorf Goodman. The white cotton drawstring bag, printed overall with *the whole works* in cherry pink, contained a little wooden stamp dispenser with all the materials to make the finished découpage box that had become so popular in the store. It was a huge success and led to several other kits for Bergdorf's.

Finally we created a line for Bloomingdale's and had a kiosk in ten stores, complete with demonstrators to show customers how to do découpage. This led to orders from such mail-order catalogs as the Horchow Collection and ultimately to J. C. Penney. It was at this point that I realized I was no longer a designer-craftsperson but a manufacturer and drowning in administrative work. It was time to sell the company and get back to what I loved best, design and writing about crafts and decorating.

Over the next twenty years my husband, Jon, and I produced more than fifty books on crafts, home style, and decorating ideas; created thousands of

This handmade lap desk, which I originally designed for Cartier, appeared in House Beautiful magazine when it was first introduced. Bright orange poppies in my yard inspired the design.

projects for magazines; and designed products for companies. Now and then I speak before women's groups. I have been attracted by many arts and crafts and have learned to do them with enough skill to teach others. But no craft has had the lasting appeal of découpage. Today my teaching is confined to television appearances and an occasional speaking engagement abroad. Writing my weekly newspaper column, "Home Style," enables me to present quick and easy decorating ideas for people who like to do things themselves.

OPPOSITE
I created this china cabinet to hold the découpage plates in my store.
ABOVE
The doors of the china cabinet are antiqued to look worn and are découpaged with a design created by cutting and piecing together prints of tall blades of grass and birds.

After twenty-five years of selling to the most sophisticated stores in the country, I now offer my work exclusively through my own store on Nantucket, where we live. Our studio is brimming with interesting objects waiting to be transformed, and the store is where they are showcased. We design everything that's used in the home, from furniture to plates. Occasionally someone who collected my original boxes stops by the store while on vacation.

My mother still does découpage as a hobby and does a great deal of cutting for me. Her technique is still and always will be better than mine. She has more patience and works on one piece at a time, creating that one jewel—as perhaps you will, too.

A HISTORY
OF DÉCOUPAGE

When my first book, *Découpage: A New Look at an Old Craft,* was published by Doubleday in 1972, not many people knew what découpage was. "Décotage? What's that?" they'd say. Or, "Décolletage? It sounds immoral," or "Déglopage? Is that a new hippie art form?" However, today everyone has heard of découpage even if he or she can't always pronounce it correctly.

Découpage (pronounced DAY-coo-pahge) is a French craft that originated in the eighteenth century. Literally translated, the word means "applied cutouts." Unlike collage, which is the technique of composing a work of art by pasting various materials not normally associated with one another on a single surface, découpage is the method of decorating an object with paper cutouts alone, usually a three-dimensional object. A découpage project is created by first cutting out paper illustrations or designs from any paper source—greeting cards, wrapping paper, calendars, wallpaper, books, even napkins or newspaper—and then arranging these cutouts in a pleasing way on an object such as a box, tray, piece of furniture, or wooden plaque. The designs might be pretty, sophisticated, whimsical, geometric, or ornate. The possibilities are endless. Once arranged, the cutouts are glued to the object and protected under many coats of a clear sealer such as varnish, polyurethane, or acrylic medium.

Découpage became quite popular for decorating all sorts of wooden boxes, furniture, and—most commonly—lunch box purses. Over the years women became more interested in filling the workplace than in filling their hours with leisure-time activities. But suddenly making something or buying something handmade is back in fashion.

A pretty grouping of découpage accessories with a rose theme on wood, glass, and ceramic.

Découpage is once again very much in vogue as a new generation of crafters is becoming aware of decorating their homes and as new materials are making the craft more accessible. With the current popularity of furnishing with flea-market and auction finds and with a new awareness of eclectic decorating with castoffs found at yard sales or forgotten treasures from our parents' attics, découpage is being rediscovered as a great way to transform the ordinary into the extraordinary.

Although découpage originated in France, it has been practiced in almost every country in the world. Fine furniture was elaborately decorated with cutouts from prints that were hand colored. Imitating the effects of freehand painting on Oriental lacquered pieces became the rage. Once the cutouts were arranged and glued to the surface, many coats of lacquer were applied to create a smooth, glasslike finish. The prints were expensive, but the people who did this craft were the wealthy elite. Because the designs were not actually painted onto the surfaces but were created from cutouts, this elitist craft was referred to ironically as *arte povero,* "the poor man's art."

During the eighteenth and nineteenth centuries découpage flourished throughout Europe and even infiltrated the court of Louis XV. Artistic ladies amused themselves by cutting out pictures and applying them to hatboxes, wig stands, fire screens, and toiletry items.

The British Museum in London has on display the work of a woman who lived in England in the early 1700s. Mary Delaney, a confidante of King George III and Queen Charlotte, produced botanically accurate reproductions of flowers cut from tissue paper that she first hand colored.

By 1730 découpage was popular in the American colonies. Despite its popularity in Boston and New York, no known pieces have survived.

In 1760 a London printer produced a book called *The Ladies Amusement, the Art of Japanning Made Easy.* This book contained 1,500 illustrations for ladies to color and cut out for use in découpage. There were also design suggestions, such as "Your designs should be balanced. For example, do not allow a butterfly to support an elephant." As the craft became more popular and printing techniques improved in America, découpeurs used cutouts from such magazines as *Godey's Lady's Book.*

In the early nineteenth century, Victorian sentimentality sparked a new impetus in découpage, coinciding with the introduction of valentine cards. Brightly colored gummed paper designs such as decals came into vogue and were used to make scrap albums. Perhaps you've seen the very ornate room-divider scrap screens that combined such decals with other prints. The gummed labels were used to decorate glass vases as well. The technique, originally called potichomanie but now referred to as reverse découpage, was intended to imitate fine porcelain. The effect was achieved by applying the glue to the front of the cutouts, which were then positioned inside the glass. White paint was then applied to the back of the print and the inside of the glass. In this case no lacquer was required. Today these antique items are considered prized collectibles.

Découpage fell out of favor in England about the time of the outbreak of World War I. In France it died out during the French Revolution and disappeared in Venice when Napoleon marched into the city. In the United States the women's movement set all crafts, especially découpage, on the back burner to simmer until the time was right for it to bubble up again. In 1972, the same year my first book on découpage was published, the National Guild of Découpeurs was formed in the United States. Its members continue to promote the art to this day.

Découpage may not be done as it was a hundred or more years ago, nor look the same. However, the same qualities that made découpage so appealing as a leisure activity in the eighteenth century still remain in the twenty-first century—the satisfaction that comes from a creative endeavor involving making something beautiful by hand. It seems fitting that a whole new generation of crafters is just now discovering découpage, proving that history does indeed repeat itself.

DÉCOUPAGE THROUGHOUT THE WORLD

- In Italy découpage was done on desks or secretaries. The treasures of the Orient strongly influenced Venetian découpeurs.

- In France Marie Antoinette and the ladies of the court became so enthusiastic over the craft that they cut up everything in sight. French découpage was very lacy and intricate and reflected the ornate character of eighteenth-century French furniture. Popular themes were flowers, butterflies, birds, cherubs, musical instruments, and garlands.

- Queen Victoria did découpage and was also a collector. A découpage screen was part of every fashionable English lady's trousseau.

- German and Austrian découpage followed the heavier look of Biedermeier furniture. The Germans used embossed scrapbook pictures of children, cherubs, and ribbons. The Germans invented the embossed printed and precut motifs, and their quality has never been surpassed.

- Swedish découpage employs the use of hand-colored earth tones on black-and-white engravings applied to dark painted backgrounds or natural dark-wood tones.

- Norwegian découpage is devoted to mythological subjects.

- In Poland, découpage is done with traditional designs executed in brightly colored paper and tinsel.

- Mexican découpage is bright and colorful and used to make holiday items.

- Belgian découpage is done with a scalpel in the manner of silhouette cutting and includes pierced work and reverse cutting.

- In Australia découpage was discovered only twenty-five years ago. They use hand-colored images, and their technique is similar to the Venetian work of the 1700s.

RIGHT

An example of an early-Victorian three-tiered table used to display framed pictures, old cars, or anything that strikes the owner's fancy.

OPPOSITE

A detail reveals the scrapbook quality of covering a surface with decals, valentines, stickers, cut paper, doilies, and cutouts in an overlapping collage of memorabilia. Gold leaf and gilt figure prominently in Victorian découpage.

2 WHAT TO DÉCOUPAGE

Before you begin to découpage a piece of furniture, consider practicing on something small such as a plaque or a box. I prefer three-dimensional objects like boxes, but I also work on flat items such as plaques and trays. A box presents many opportunities to learn the technique as well as how to design. You'll find unfinished boxes at large craft stores along with all the materials needed.

However, if you prefer jumping into the deep end of the pool and have inherited from a great-aunt a wonderful old bureau that just needs some loving care to restore it, this is perhaps the way to go. When working on a piece that is especially dear to you, the process is more meaningful and the project may even become an heirloom. My favorite objects to

découpage are the unusual pieces I find at yard sales, auctions, flea markets (especially abroad), and antique or secondhand stores. I visit a handful of funky little out-of-the-way shops in different towns, which gives meaning to my travels.

The best way to decide what to découpage is to think about what you need. Will the object be used in a specific room? Will it serve a useful purpose? Will it be a gift? If you know beforehand why you want to make a découpage piece, you'll ultimately be better able to choose its colors and design.

PREVIOUS SPREAD

There is an endless supply of interesting pieces to découpage. When you find something you like, try to assess how much prep work is needed and if you are up to the challenge.

OPPOSITE

Ready-to-finish boxes and découpage material can be found in most craft stores. Choose large cutouts such as fruit for a first project. The fine cutting required for flowers is more difficult.

RIGHT

A box makes a good first project for learning technique and how to design.

OLD VS. NEW

I have always been a fan of ready-to-finish furniture. It is a blank canvas, with no particular inherent beauty, just waiting to be transformed. Unlike finding a used dresser at a yard sale, there is no old finish to strip or nicks and scratches to repair before beginning. If I'm looking for a basic chest of drawers, a toy chest, or a plain wooden barstool, I can usually find one in ready-to-finish furniture. I often buy small step stools to découpage with various themes.

However, ready-to-finish furniture has some inherent problems. Unfinished-furniture outlets are not always easy to find, and the pieces are very basic in design. Most unfinished furniture is also made of soft pine, which doesn't have the quality of hardwood and is crudely made. Starting with an inferior product isn't the best way to turn out a superior finished piece. Further, pine usually has knots in the surface that will show through whatever finish coats them. A shellac sealer can be used on bare wood before painting; two or three primer coats stave off discoloration from the knots that would eventually begin to bleed through the top coats of paint. However, shellac sealer cannot be used under wood stain.

Many of the better furniture pieces that we découpage in the studio, such as dining tables, are made of alder, a hardwood that comes from the Northwest. Once in a while I find a nice piece of furniture made of oak, and on occasion I work on maple furniture.

Secondhand furniture has its problems as well. Most old furniture is coated with lacquer or shellac, both of which were used before varnish and polyurethane were invented. Even if you aren't sure about the finish, chances are that the item has been waxed or coated with something that may not interact well with your découpage materials and must be removed. To do so is not difficult but is time-consuming. It's best to look for wooden objects that are free of shellac or another coating.

With all the problems one finds in secondhand furniture, I still favor it over new, unfinished pieces. For one thing, you can always find the unusual or a piece that has character

LEFT
Ready-to-finish furniture is usually made of pine, which requires two or three coats of sealer to cover unsightly knots in the wood before painting. (See page 6 for finished piece.)
ABOVE
A sampling of good basic pieces for a découpage design. (See page 177 for finished toy chest.)

or something from the past that exudes history. Often these pieces require renovation, overhaul, or some sort of fixing, but they can be worth the trouble.

I don't have nearly enough time to spend scouring the countryside for interesting odds and ends to découpage. It makes me envious when I read about a part of the country where flea markets and auctions are a way of life. In the Northeast the most famous outdoor event of this sort is held twice a year in Brimfield, Massachusetts. Dealers and buyers make their travel arrangements a year in advance, and this event covers several miles of outdoor display space. More than five thousand vendors participate. I find it far too daunting to attempt to plow through acres of stuff in search of just the right items. I prefer a more edited,

SPICE CABINET (OLD FURNITURE)

Any found object poses a design challenge—this is what makes découpage forever interesting. This charming item came out of a curiosity shop but was obviously a garage-made project by a home hobbyist. It probably once held spices in the kitchen, but it can be used in an office to hold desktop items, or in the bathroom to organize cosmetics and hair clips. Or it can just be a sweet little accessory to hang on a wall or display on a shelf.

The wood is very thick, the precision of the angles isn't quite perfect, and the individual drawers are quite chunky. It was already covered with several coats of white paint, and I decided to leave it that way. This item reminds me of the boxes my grandfather used to make in his garage for my first découpage projects. These boxes, made from scraps of wood or even wooden slats from old Venetian blinds, usually revealed imperfections in the wood as well as in the construction.

To offset the crudeness of the wood, I decided to use a delicate design. The bright red poppies were perfect against the antiseptic white background, like cherries in the snow. Once I thought the design on the cabinet was complete, I stepped back and realized it didn't look quite finished. I searched through my bird guidebooks and found a bird with just a little spot of red on its breast, and more important, it was the right size to fit the space. I always line the insides of pieces with pretty paper that includes an accent color found on the outside design, adding an element of surprise. In this case, heavy red wrapping paper with a bird-and-vine motif in a subtler shade of red complemented the reddish orange of the poppies beautifully. The paper is thicker than ordinary gift-wrap paper, which made it better for use as a liner.

Yard sales, flea markets, auctions, and antique shops offer possibilities for finding more unusual pieces to découpage. However, these pieces often require sanding or refinishing before they are ready for the découpage process.

One of my favorite places to find unusual things with a decidedly European flavor is the weekend street fair in L'Isle-sur-la-Sorgue, a town in the south of France.

manageable way of finding things. Local auctions, secondhand shops, antique stores, and yard sales are my venues of choice, along with occasional trips to flea markets and antiquarian-print shows abroad.

Unusual objects make wonderful découpage accessories, as they add the element of surprise to any decor. Forage carefully; most of these castoffs are easy to overlook if you aren't thinking creatively. It could be just an ordinary wooden bowl that you wouldn't dream of using to serve salad. However, as a découpage project it might be beautiful filled with potpourri on your holiday table. My friend Ann Killen, owner of a closet-size shop crammed with found objects, is such a good saleswoman that she actually sold me a big wooden truck with a hole in the top. It's been sitting in the studio for over a year waiting for a good idea. I'm sure there's not another one like it.

STEP STOOLS: SIX DESIGNS (NEW FURNITURE)

A basic, unfinished step stool is a good example of the versatility of ready-to-finish furniture; the flat area provides a great canvas on which to create a découpage design. Here are six different versions of the same item to show the various design possibilities.

A simple flag motif on a white background is a wonderful graphic symbol.

An illustration cut from an early children's nursery book.

Peter Rabbit cutouts decorate this personalized stool.

Cut lemon prints on a yellow background.

Wallpaper cutouts on a blue background.

Purple and blue hydrangeas always look pretty on a white background.

YARD-SALE FINDS

All across America yard sales are at the top of the A-rated leisure-time activities. Whether we need more "stuff" or not, we scour the classified section of the paper and circle the yard sales of interest. For some, making the rounds of yard sales is part of a Saturday morning ritual. Yard sales are great ways to see different parts of your hometown, or even a town you might be visiting. We peek into our neighbors' houses, chitchat with acquaintances, exchange pleasantries with perfect strangers who after a few such Saturday encounters become fast friends, and spend an hour or two outdoors. Best of all, there is always the chance of finding something worth turning into a découpage project.

How many old bureaus and chairs have been given a new lease on life with a coat of paint, a decorative finish, and a little tender loving care by a second or third owner? What a great system we have for recycling in this country!

Several years ago *Woman's Day* magazine commissioned our studio to decorate a beachside cottage with yard-sale and auction finds along with some unfinished furniture makeovers. It took an

OPPOSITE
A kitchen chair found at a yard sale is painted blue and given a whimsical découpage design with cut-up wrapping paper.
RIGHT
Originally longer, the legs of the table were cut down to make it fit in front of the sofa. The wooden hutch was a ready-to-finish piece that we stained and filled with nautical-related crafts: a model sailboat, carved shorebirds by Ray Freden, sailors' valentines made with shells, and Nantucket lightship baskets.

entire summer and was one of the best projects we ever undertook. When we started, the cottage was completely empty. Each week we attended yard sales with a checklist in hand. We found a wonderful eclectic mix of pieces, some of which we painted; others we covered with fabric, and a few we transformed with découpage.

The main living space looked out onto beach grass and sand dunes and the ocean beyond, so we chose a nautical theme and used it throughout the room. A navigational survey map was the découpage motif for the top of the coffee table, found at a yard sale. Painted seafoam green to match the background of the map, this object became the focal point of the room. The fabric used to re-cover the cushions on the found bamboo sofa reflects the dune grass, weeds, and flowers growing around the house.

The kitchen is a good place to experiment and have fun with decorative finishes. I love sprinkling yellow with a blue and white color scheme for the kitchen. Even now, several years after we originally designed the room, the colors look fresh and uplifting together. Kitchen chairs are the single most discarded pieces of furniture offered at yard sales. It doesn't matter if they match or not. Once we had amassed six chairs in approximately the same size, they were given a new life with bright blue paint and a sponged finish. They fit perfectly around the ready-to-finish farm table.

All the accessories came from yard sales as well. If the dishes are in the same color family, it doesn't matter if they match. A bowl filled with ripe lemons or a pitcher holding a bouquet of freshly cut flowers is all it takes to brighten up a breakfast table. The filmy hospital-thrift-shop curtains were pinned up at one corner for a decidedly casual, beach-cottage feeling. During the day the curtains may be left open to reveal the view as the ocean breeze blows freely through the house; at night the windows can be covered easily.

Laura Ashley wallpaper is used as a decorative border around the top of a ready-to-finish kitchen farm table. An unfinished jelly cupboard in the corner is painted white and stenciled with a matching blue border design. Mismatched kitchen chairs look good together with a blue sponge-painted finish. (See "Special Effects," page 182.)

AUCTION FEVER

Auctions present great opportunities for finding old and interesting objects to découpage. It is fun to see the sorts of furnishings that come out of local homes. In fact, most of my rooms are furnished with auction purchases that have contributed to an eclectic style that, when I'm in a generous mood, I think looks rather charming. It's an unplanned style that simply evolved.

Auctions and yard sales are my answer to mall shopping and just as much fun. I sat through one auction and wondered what my friend Tom had in mind for a life-size Egyptian mummy case he bought. Mary Beth, in the seat next to me, bid on a lovely blue and white china container that now holds red geraniums in front of her art gallery, and I got a crude, extremely heavy lingerie dresser that looked as though it had potential for a découpage project. We did not go to the auction seeking those specific items, but we all felt as though we had found an unexpected prize at the bottom of the Cracker Jack box.

Buying at auction takes practice and patience. It is not a place to be impulsive. However, come ready to make decisions quickly, as auctions definitely are not for procrastinators. I have spent many hours watching all sorts of items come up for sale that I later wished I had bid on. Deliberation has no place at an auction.

All auctions have a preview time. It pays to take this opportunity to inspect the items that will come up for sale, as you may not see imperfections from your seat. Determine what you want to bid on, set a price, and resolve not to go above it. Know that if you pay more for an item than you decided it was worth, you will kick yourself. Of course, if you get it for less, you'll be forever addicted to auction buying. You may find yourself scratching your head and questioning your sanity as you wrestle an oversize chair into an undersize car. Or you may find your neighbors staring wistfully at your largesse of a coat rack, albeit with a

The bright yellow and blue pattern in the wallpaper is carried out through the rest of the kitchen with plates, bowls, and napkins. A simple bowl of ripe lemons and a pitcher filled with fresh flowers make a breakfast table special.

few missing pegs, a wobbly table, and a bureau whose drawers are forever stuck shut, wishing they had gotten there first.

What really keeps those seats filled at local auctions is the suspense. What will be offered? What will I bid? Will I get it? And finally, the thrill of taking it home and finding a place to display or use it, then the enjoyment of living with it. And what could be more fun than to turn someone else's castoff into a découpage treasure?

Lingerie Dresser

This lingerie dresser is just the sort of item you can find at a local auction. It has nice proportions and can be used in a variety of ways. Since it is tall and narrow, it can fit against an otherwise unused wall space. The deep drawers make it practical for holding lingerie in a

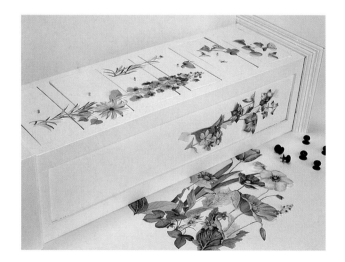

bedroom, or odds and ends in a bathroom. Since the dresser already had a coat of ivory paint, maybe even several coats, the piece needed only to be lightly sanded, have a few small nicks filled in, and given one last coat of paint to render it ready for découpage. However, the size presented a design problem. A strip of leftover wallpaper was the perfect solution. It provided a colorful pattern of tall flowers to cut out and rearrange on the dresser.

ABOVE AND OPPOSITE
This tall lingerie dresser, purchased at an auction, required large cutouts to fit on the long, narrow shape. Flowers from leftover wallpaper create this design. For this project it was necessary to cut out all the illustrations and then re-create them to fit the shape and size of the dresser. Some of the stems had to be elongated, and some flowers were pieced together to make them "grow" naturally up the sides and over the drawers. The inside of the dresser drawers could be lined with scented lining paper or with paper in a color that matches one of the flowers in the découpage design. Painted wooden knobs, decorated with a little hydrangea or rose petal cutout, replace the old knobs. Lavender and blue hydrangeas encircle the flower caddy sitting on top of the dresser and tie in with the découpage knobs, as if the blossoms had been plucked from the larger flowers for this purpose.

3 VISUAL INSPIRATION

I AM OFTEN ASKED where I get my ideas for découpage. My answer is "Everywhere!" My life is one in which I am always seeing things in relation to my work. A woman might walk into my shop wearing a floral-print shirt and I see it cut up and rearranged on an object. I especially like to poke around in little boutiques that feature unusual gift items. Something always gives me an idea. I love walking through the home-furnishings department of better stores such as Harrods in London, where I can't resist thinking about art deco designs. One year I stumbled upon vases with a crackle finish in the home-furnishings department of Neiman Marcus in Dallas and spent the better part of a month learning the technique, only to decide I didn't really like it. Almost any better boutique offers me creative input. A red silk scarf on a mannequin in a store window on the Upper East Side of Manhattan once caught my eye and I knew I had to paint a project with that exact tomato red color.

Home-design catalogs arrive daily, and I pore over them all. I look to see what colors are predicted to become the season's most popular. I check out texture and design and style. Hand-dyed velvet pillows in soft, sun-soaked colors such as sienna and tangerine inspire me to use these colors as painted backgrounds. Roses woven into Egyptian cotton duvet covers suggest a delicate design for little bathroom containers. Pillowcases embroidered with a scalloped edge remind me that doilies are fun to découpage onto round coasters. Pure white soap in the shape of pebbles and shells seem like good design motifs for a variety of containers for the bathroom or a beach house.

When choosing a down comforter, just the mention of its Scandinavian roots gives it an immediate stamp of approval. But more than a desire for the comforter is my interest in the furniture on which it is displayed. The hand-rubbed white finish on country beds and the blue and white painted trim on armoires holding those cloud-soft covers make me want to start a new project with a decidedly Swedish influence. Scandinavian stylebooks take over where the catalogs leave off, and I immerse myself in that country's design influences before I get going. It might be weeks, even months, before I am sure what it is I would like to make, but the ideas are germinating and filed in my head for future use.

PREVIOUS SPREAD
A Nantucket lightship basket is filled with a summer bouquet.

OPPOSITE
Unfinished-wood trinket boxes are sanded, painted, decorated with cut-out designs, and coated with many layers of sealer until smooth to the touch.

"Where do you get your cutouts?" is another familiar question. I have collected botanical prints for thirty years and have a studio filled with material to draw upon. Lovely old prints, illustrated books, greeting cards, books, calendars, art prints, printed material sold in craft stores specifically for this purpose, even wrapping paper, are all excellent sources for découpage material. However, I never recommend magazines as a source of material. The paper wrinkles when glued to a surface and once the paper is covered with sealer, the print often shows through from the underside. Now and then the printing smears when coated with sealer.

OPPOSITE AND ABOVE
Handmade boxes with whimsical illustrations from an early nursery book series.

It seems hard to believe but when I started decoupage, color copying wasn't readily available, so I cut up original material. Only occasionally do I make color copies of the prints I intend to use. I prefer the pieces I découpage to be unique, and I often cut up an entire book or an original print for my work. I especially do so when I'm working on something that I know will be sold in the store, or something that's a special order for someone's home. I like my work to be something you won't find anywhere else. It's worth noting that printed pieces fade over time when exposed to direct sunlight. I know it seems foolhardy to use original material, but I work on so many projects at one time that I don't like to repeat myself. The reality is that for me, creating new projects is what keeps me interested in the craft.

FLOWERS

No single element is more influential in my work than flowers. I have always used flower prints to cut up for découpage. This is the way the French originated the craft, and it appeals to my sense of design. The possibilities are limitless, illustrations are readily available, and whatever you put them on, the finished project looks good. Flowers as a design motif work with every decorating style and always add pretty touches.

CLOCKWISE FROM TOP

All summer, rose-covered cottages create a fairy-tale setting.

Tropical flowers are hard to ignore as a design motif. Take inspiration from your own garden or indigenous flowers in your area.

Exotic orchids abound in southern climates and offer inspiration for découpage projects.

Black-eyed Susans grow in profusion behind a painted gate.

Roses

Roses represent the quintessential image captured by artists for centuries. Illustrations are plentiful, whether in the form of an artist's print, on wrapping paper, as gift cards, or in books. I use this flower more than any other in my découpage projects. Every year I go to London to buy Victorian rose prints, and I make a line of limited-edition rose plates every summer to present in my shop. Each is of a different rose in different colors. Since I have a passion for setting a pretty table, I especially like to overdo it with roses.

ABOVE
Roses have always been the inspiration for artists and designers. They probably represent the most popular design in home furnishing products.
RIGHT
A group of my découpage boxes with rose motifs. These are a few of the boxes my grandfather made for me many years ago. I continue to work on them and make only a handful each year.

A BRIDAL SHOWER WITH A ROSE THEME

Any party, whether for a bride-to-be or to celebrate a birthday, can be made special with a beautiful table setting. All it takes is a decorating theme. A rose motif suggests femininity and romance, so it's best to keep all the accessories light and airy. Layering linens such as an antique crocheted tablecloth over a pale pink tablecloth gives the table a lush look. Linen place mats are adorned with hand-painted roses. The plates are marbleized with gold paint and covered with ivory-colored enamel. The image on each plate is a basket of pink roses; the same flowers are used to decorate a napkin/silverware caddy. A miniature basket holding a tiny bouquet of roses is placed at each setting.

More découpage roses decorate a small wooden tray that could hold mints or favors for the bridesmaids. An art deco silver creamer holds a bunch of fresh roses, and I tucked one rose under the ribbon tied around each pink napkin. It's fun to use interesting objects for holding flowers, even if that wasn't their original purpose. The pièce de résistance is the rose-covered gazebo, which was originally black and dirty and screaming to be rescued.

For a last detail I added a small, delicately printed pillow on each of the chairs. Pink glasses and floral prints on the walls add to the overall theme.

Sunflowers and Poppies

One year we rented a house high above the Vaucluse Valley in the south of France. It was springtime and every morning we looked out over our balcony to the fields of mustard and sunflowers growing below. Everything was a blanket of yellow. I could see how difficult it would be to ignore the sunflower as an image to illustrate. I went looking for prints of sunflowers. They were not hard to find.

Once I started looking for sunflowers, my antennae were up for this design. One Sunday I was poking through a rather scant flea market when I found a stack of old children's books, one of which had illustrations of poppies and sunflowers bordering each page. For one dollar I had a gold mine of potential cutouts. These designs are small enough to use on my

LEFT

A large sunflower poster proves the right size to fit on a painted electrical spool to use as a garden table.

OPPOSITE

A narrow deck provides a place to catch the morning sun just off the master bedroom and bath of this Key West home (see page 98). Sunflowers in a stone vase inspired the design for the gold découpage plate. This assemblage is made up of different shapes, textures, and heights. Water trickles from the stone sculpture, adding another dimension—sound.

FOLLOWING SPREAD

I designed a tray, step stool, and table with a sunflower motif. The table has a wrought-iron frame with a set-in glass top. The découpage is applied to the underside of the glass. This is one of my series of pressed-flower prints (see page 122, "A Colorful Setting," for other projects). The green tin is sponge-painted and découpaged with crocus cutouts.

Bright pink or orange poppy petals are easy to press for use in découpage. Art prints in all sizes can be found to use on everything from small boxes to large pieces of furniture.

little 3-inch round "trinket" boxes. I also used these flowers to cover one of the shoe lasts I collect (see page 191). If you know what projects you like to work on, it's easier to find illustrations to match.

Another thing I like to do when traveling is pick a flower growing in the area to press in my journal. On a trip down the Canal du Midi we pulled our barge up to the bank and secured it with a rope around a tree right next to a cluster of bright orange poppies. These flowers are so lovely and delicate and when growing in a patch are dramatic to behold. The petals I pressed ultimately turned deep purple in the process, but the image of these vibrant flowers inspired many future projects, and I am still, years later, enamored of the poppy as a découpage design element. I look for them whenever I am in an antique-print shop or bookstore. When used on a stark white painted background, the bright red/orange petals and the intensely green leaves are a winning combination.

OPPOSITE
These boxes are the perfect size to hold pens and pencils on a desk. The graceful curves of the tulips soften the severe lines of the box.

Tulips

Though not as celebrated as the daffodil, tulips have been heralded for centuries as a universal symbol of spring. According to the Netherlands Tulip Association, there are more than five hundred varieties of cut tulips available today. The choices are endless, as tulips come in all hues, both soft and brilliant: red, pink, yellow, purple, orange, white, lavender, and bicolored.

Some tulips are surprisingly exotic, with fringed or ruffled edges. Floral designers report that for pure romance, ruffled parrot tulips are beginning to challenge roses as a Valentine's Day gift. I prefer the large French tulips in the palest shades of peach or white.

DECORATING WITH TULIPS

- Color talks. Make a statement with one color.

- Buy the tulips with flower buds closed but just ready to open.

- Before arranging tulips, condition them by recutting the base of the stem with a clean sharp knife. Cut straight across the stem, not at a slant. This will open the flower's water uptake channels. Advice from the Tulip Association: "Forget those cut-flower food packets, tulips are self-sufficient."

- Tulips are particularly thirsty. Check the water level daily. Refresh or change the water every day for the longest vase life.

- Unlike most flowers, tulips keep growing in the vase—sometimes as much as an inch or more after being arranged. The result: tulips have the rare ability to move or dance in the vase. Don't expect them to just stand there, stiff and upright. Tulips will bend and twist to their own delight—and yours, a trait treasured by floral designers. Remember this when designing your découpage projects. Don't use only stiff flowers. Try to curve the stems to create a graceful design. This whimsical bending is actually caused by the dual effects of continued stem growth and the gentle pull of light and gravity on the flower head.

- Tulips, like daisies (another one of my découpage favorites), look at home in any type of container, from the homeliest tin can to the most elegant vase. I like red tulips in a white country pitcher or white tulips in a clear glass vase. A bowl filled with any color and set into a basket is another winner.

- With proper care, tulips should open and last from five to seven days. Keep them away from sources of heat.

- When the stems begin to droop but the petals haven't yet begun to shed, cut the stems quite short and make a tight little bouquet in a basket in order to extend the enjoyment right to the bitter end.

- To make a bouquet of tulips last forever, cut them from paper illustrations to use on a box, vase, furniture, lampshade, or plant holder. Use the real bouquet for design and placement inspiration.

My collection of tulips and exotic flowers in shades of orange and yellow with bright green leaves and stems proved a winning match with the original butterscotch color of this bed tray. Although the paint was chipped and the gold rim was rather worn, I loved the color and could hardly hope to match the original if I sanded down to the bare wood and repainted it, so I decided to leave it as is. That it isn't perfect adds to its charm. The owners of this home couldn't resist styling the tray with a vintage incense burner in the form of a woman smoking a cigarette. All that was needed were the glasses of cool drinks to be brought poolside.

Nasturtium

Bright yellow and orange nasturtium in huge pots dot the gray deck with color in front of my friend Judy's house. Each morning when I walked by, I was struck by the brilliance of these flowers in the morning sunlight. I imagined using this design for all sorts of items, from planters to plates. I imagined what color I would paint the background. By the time I found just the right items to découpage, I knew the nasturtium would look best against burnt orange or light gray for decidedly different looks.

A treasure box is painted light gray and decorated with nasturtium cutouts that are arranged to conform to the curved shape. The box is lined with bright orange paper. The entire box is antiqued to make it look old.

Daffodils

Daffodils are the exalted symbol of spring. There is nothing quite as cheerful as a mason jar filled with yellow daffys on the kitchen counter. Suddenly everything smells better and looks fresher, and the bright yellow color is the prettiest ever. That's all it takes to transform a stuffy room after the long winter months: simple, inexpensive, and brimming with country charm.

I found this old picnic basket in a local antique shop. It was in good condition, and although the wooden top needed sanding to make it smooth and clean, once it was covered with the yellow paint, it presented the perfect surface for a découpage design. The daffodils were blooming everywhere and inspired me to cover the lid with this spring motif. One flower was placed on the underside of the lid, so it is just as pretty open as closed.

Hydrangeas

What is it about hydrangeas? Everyone loves them, especially here in the Northeast. Because Nantucket is so small and gardens tend to surround in-town houses right to the street, they are abundantly obvious and seem to bloom all at once.

The bushes, which blossom in the summer, are overwhelmingly beautiful. No tourist can resist taking pictures of them or placing their subjects in front of them. Those who have hydrangea bushes growing in their yards cut them routinely for exquisite bouquets. It takes only two or three to make a nice arrangement, especially when the blossoms are full. Their colors seem right at home in any room. In the fall, islanders cut the fading blossoms to make wreaths.

I think of the hydrangea as an all-American flower. However, they are just as popular in England and continental Europe. When I was in Italy I happened into a little print shop where I discovered two similar watercolor prints, one each of a lavender and blue hydrangea.

"How many of these do you have?" I asked the proprietor. "About a hundred," she answered. "I'll take them all" was my reply. You can imagine my euphoria. I use them on everything from my plates to furniture.

The hydrangea is a wonderful design motif for all sorts of craft projects. A border of blue and lavender hydrangeas interspersed with bright green leaves is a lovely way to enhance a room; an old dresser can be transformed with a fresh coat of white paint and hydrangeas découpaged

ABOVE
Wallpaper hydrangea cutouts can be used for a découpage project such as this large wooden tray.
OPPOSITE
An unfinished drop-leaf table with a pretty shape lends itself to a continuous border of hydrangeas with alternating blue and pink blossoms. I used two of the flowers on the center top and another one on the bottom shelf.

across the drawers. I use the hydrangea theme on floorcloths, small dressers, lampshades, wooden accessories of all kinds, and especially the plates that have become my signature item.

Plates, Trays, and Accessories Hydrangeas come in many shades of blue, lavender, wine, and, in rare cases, white. The beautiful periwinkle blue is perhaps the most common and the most popular. It is said that the color of a plant has much to do with the acidity of the soil and that a gardener with some knowledge can effectively add chemicals to control the color. I have blue hydrangea bushes in my yard and I love using them in arrangements all summer long. I also love to press the individual blossoms for découpage projects.

ABOVE

A softer version of hydrangeas in pastel colors is used for accents in a white bedroom. The découpage plate on the wall is decorated with a pink hydrangea and backed with a mauve-colored rice paper; the carryall is decorated with blossoms on each side for a continuous design all around. This is a good example of how découpage can be used to create a theme on many different surfaces: a lampshade, cabinet, carryall, and plate hanging on the wall. In this case, I chose the lavender color for the plate background to match the color of the mohair throw.

OPPOSITE TOP

I painted this pine wheelbarrow ivory, then covered it all around with cut-out prints of hydrangea blossoms and leaves. This is an outdoor project; however, it would be just as lovely on a screened porch or other protected outdoor area.

CONTAINERS

When filling containers with hydrangeas, more is certainly better. Baskets, tins, crocks, pitchers, glass vases, and mason jars are but a few of the holders I love to use. My current favorite is a white enamel measuring cup that holds four to six blossoms. Look around your house for anything to turn into a creative flower container. You'll be surprised how good almost anything looks holding these beauties.

4 DESIGN

OAXACA

MARK HAMPTON ON DECORATING

THE ARTS+CRAFTS LIFESTYLE AND DESIGN

VILLAGES OF ENGLAND Richard Turpin · Roger Hunt

HULL
BARNARD

MY APPROACH
TO DESIGN

I am a designer at heart, with no formal training in art. However, I come from an artistic family. My mother and grandparents introduced me to a creative lifestyle, and I have lived and worked with a professional designer for more than thirty years. How my husband sees things influenced me in a way that no formal education could have. When I am unsure about whether a design is working, I rely on his judgment before making a final decision. We have evolved into a symbiotic team.

Découpage is the medium through which I express my sense of design. My work is about the beauty of the illustrations and how they can be manipulated to integrate seamlessly with the shape and size of the object to which they are applied. The secondary considerations are the materials and end use of the project. I am less interested in the technique of découpage than in the decisions that go into the design process. However, you have to learn the technique so you can do it flawlessly; then it becomes second nature and the tool through which your designs come to life.

When I began selling my work, my target audience was high-end stores whose customers would appreciate handmade goods. For this reason I have had to strive for a level of professionalism that goes beyond simply pleasing myself. The customers who come into my store have discerning taste— which is good because it challenges me. The world is fashion-driven, and most design is short-lived and disposable. New

OPPOSITE
Roses, anemones, and poppies suggested the color scheme for a bright corner of my living room. I painted an occasional table with bright cherry red enamel and placed it under a print of poppies. The large tin lamp is painted the same red color, but the finish is matte rather than glossy. A découpage platter of anemones has a green painted background that picks up the color of the cut paper leaves on the découpage box as well as the color of the real leaves of the plant. A red Oriental area rug warms the room and picks up the red accent colors.

ABOVE
Window boxes brimming with flowers are a Nantucket staple on houses, storefronts, and public buildings all over town.

design ideas are always in demand, and this takes time and attention and being up on trends. Also, I have grown as a designer, having created thousands of pieces over the years. Looking back, some of my original projects seem charmingly naïve. I feel fortunate to have had the opportunity to keep improving on my technique as well as my design style.

My educational background is in journalism. I became proficient at a variety of popular crafts and used them to apply my design and writing skills to a general audience. I have been writing a weekly newspaper column on home design for more than twenty years and have authored hundreds of how-to features for magazines as well as dozens of craft books for every skill level and taste. This experience taught me that the way to most people's hearts is with a pretty object. Pretty makes us feel good. *Pretty,* according to my Oxford English Dictionary, means "pleasing or attractive in a graceful or delicate way" and is synonymous with *beautiful.* When used with *up,* as to "pretty up," we know exactly what we mean.

As a designer I am more comfortable with curves than with straight lines, so flowers suit my sense of aesthetics. Occasionally I design with geometric shapes such as postcards and invitations or announcements. I also use flag symbols in many of my designs. When I need inspiration, or when I've been staring at a blank tabletop for too long without a clue as to what I should put on it, I go for a walk. I find inspiration everywhere I turn, from the ocean to the historic buildings to the incredibly beautiful flowers and nature of Nantucket that play prominently in my work.

For a few years I taught découpage aboard the *Queen Elizabeth 2* cruise ship. The most outstanding thing I learned from that experience is that if sixty men and women are given the same printed material and the same wooden boxes, at the end of a week you will have sixty completely different finished boxes. Each person looked at his or her materials and arranged them in a way that was appealing to that individual. I learned as much from my students as they did from me.

Wherever you live, wherever you travel, there is inspiration all around you. Finding a design direction for a découpage project is simply a matter of being aware. You can teach yourself to look at the world differently, becoming aware of details, and this will be reflected in the projects you create.

DESIGN THEMES

Designing a découpage project is like making a patchwork quilt. You always need twice as many cutouts as you end up using. It takes several tries at moving the elements around within the allotted space to come up with a design that fits the background in size and color and is pleasing to the eye. If you are unsure about a layout, the best advice is to trust your instincts. Designing a project should be fun, not agony. When you think your design layout looks good, do not hesitate—use it. You can easily move things around until the design looks better to you. With each project you gain confidence, so if you start with something small, you cannot make too big a mistake.

Since I use flowers for most of my découpage projects, I often use them as my theme. For example, when I set a table in the summertime, I often use a blue and white color scheme with blue hydrangeas as the dominant theme. I have used this image to make a set of plates and frequently fill a basket with hydrangeas for my centerpiece. Flowers present an obvious design direction, but there are many other possibilities for a découpage project. The theme might be nostalgia, holidays, colors, fruits and vegetables—or anything that works within your decorating scheme.

Patriotic

The American flag has become a popular motif in many different crafts. Aside from evoking patriotic feelings, the graphic design and colors of the flag are dramatic and go well with many interior design decorations. For example, an occasional table with a découpage flag design will be right at home with blue or red checked fabric for a country look. A quilted flag pillow in a white environment looks quite contemporary.

ABOVE

On July 4 flags are hung on historic houses in Nantucket.

LEFT

Mailboxes such as this one, found in a novelty store, are perfect for a patriotic theme. The boxes had a painted design on the front that was sanded away; the boxes were then repainted in Colonial blue. A flag design on the front works beautifully with the star-shaped cutout at the top. Once the boxes were sufficiently sanded and painted, I found a book of flags on sale at a local bookstore. When creating a design, it helps to have more cutouts than you'll end up using. This way, you have options for creating the final design.

RIGHT
This mailbox is coated with many layers of polyurethane to protect it from the elements.

BELOW
Once I finished the mailboxes, I was hooked on the patriotic theme and began looking for other items to découpage. I used a simple but brightly colored flag from a brochure sent to me several years ago in the center of a painted stool used as a desk accessory for holding a plant. Jon takes many photographs of flags hanging from Nantucket homes, and I chose one of my favorites to go with my patriotic theme. Rounding out this scene is one of my framed quilted fabric flags.

Many artists and crafters use flags as the inspiration for their work. Printed flags from other countries, boat signal flags, and state flags can be used as decorative elements in découpage projects. A bicentennial flag is another design motif around which to create a project.

If you're designing a tray or a tabletop, for example, you might begin by assembling a variety of flags or different American flags of the same size. Find an image of a flag that fits well on the top of a table and then look for a border to use around the outer rim, serving as a frame for the center design.

Shells

Seashells are wonderful motifs for many découpage projects. Sometimes I use the natural-colored, realistic illustrations and sometimes I use blue stylized cutouts. Shells come in many different colors and shapes and provide endless inspiration for designing découpage projects to use in the summertime.

LEFT
A bathroom is accessorized with a shell motif. I used wallpaper with a blue and white shell motif to cut out images for the caddy/organizer, the lampshade, a shelf, and a little step stool to hold a plant.

RIGHT
Seashells provide endless inspiration for découpage projects. I use the scallop shell often because it represents the scallop industry here on Nantucket and because its shape is so pretty and graceful.

ENTERTAINING WITH A SHELL THEME

- Fill four inexpensive glass candleholders with a variety of beach shells. Then fill the glasses with water and top them with small round white floating candles.

- Scatter a few shells over the table around the candleholders.

- Add white or sand-colored place mats and napkins and you have a simple outdoor dining setting.

Fruits and Veggies

Fruits and vegetables are easy shapes to cut out and are obvious choices as a motif for plates and kitchen accessories such as a step stool or a recipe box. I make many dessert plates with images of fruit and I use vegetables on my hors d'oeuvres plates. The round shapes of the fruits and vegetables lend themselves to the shape and size of the plate.

Large glass bowls work particularly well with a variety of whole and sliced fruit. A watermelon print is the perfect shape for the bottom of the bowl. I often use it as a summertime design motif because I love the bright pink and lime green color combination as well as its shape. The cutouts are applied

OPPOSITE
I found prints of fruit and vegetables in Italy that became the basis for a line of plates I make for my store. The dark green background and gold marbleizing give them a Tuscan flavor. The back of each plate is finished with marbleized gold and black paper. Several coats of sealer render them safe for use, but they must be washed by hand.

LEFT
The same fruits used again to cover a step stool. You can't overdo a good thing! Many coats of glossy sealer protect the découpage design so the stool is resistant to wear and tear.

on the outside of the glass so you see them from inside the bowl. When the design is complete and the fruit cutouts surround the bowl, cover the surface with green enamel paint and finish it with decorative paper or tissue. I like to think of these pieces as "surreal"; once the real fruit salad (for which the bowl is used) is consumed, the fruit still remains in the bowl. Small, 7-inch plates for dessert are each découpaged with a print of a different fruit, always including a slice of watermelon.

An alternative to a bowl full of fruit is a bowl filled with vegetables. You'll find illustrations of fruit and vegetables for this purpose on greeting cards, on wrapping paper, and in books.

ABOVE

Tangerines and lemons—whole, cut, and peeled—are applied to a wooden recipe box. These are the same fruit prints that I used on the plates.

OPPOSITE

Cutouts of whole and sliced pieces of fruit are applied to the outside of a glass bowl. Green enamel paint, paper, and many coats of sealer follow. The bowl in back is filled with real fruit. An individual dessert plate is backed with rice paper. Working on any curved glass surface is perhaps the hardest découpage project. I recommend that you work on flat glass before attempting a project such as this.

A GOOD IDEA

A few of my customers tell me they collect watermelon accessories. It might be an appliqué on a pillow, a folk art wood carving, or a framed picture. Make a folk art wall hanging to add a playful note to your home. Cut out a picture of a slice of watermelon and découpage it onto a rough wooden plaque or a kitchen chair.

Travel

A piece that serves as a reminder of a trip, a meaningful experience, or a happy occasion is a decorative accessory that will personalize your home—and it makes a good gift. It is fun to collect découpage material while traveling. Different regions often carry products with images of the area. I always collect paper memorabilia such as postcards, a local newspaper (especially in a foreign language), napkins, and theater stubs. You do not have to know how they will be used, but you will be happy to have this collection of things to inspire you when you get home.

I have a collection of old island postcards that I like to use on tables and trays. When designing with geometric shapes, I have to ask myself, "Do I line them up symmetrically, or do I place them on an angle? Do I integrate them with other elements to soften the sharp edges?" I like to soften straight edges of a motif by overlapping cutouts onto the design—in this case, the postcards. The entire design is thereby integrated, rather than all the elements being plunked down in place, unrelated to one another.

Postcards present their own unique problems for découpage. They are too thick to use as is, whether with other elements or alone. It takes more than thirty coats to cover them so that the object can be used. Paper this thick requires thinning. To do so, you must peel a layer of paper away from the back of the postcard. Cover the back of the postcard with clear packing tape and smooth it down with the edge of a credit card or similar item. Carefully pull the tape away and with it will come a layer of paper from the back of the postcard. This method is not always successful on the first try. If the paper is removed in some areas but not others, you'll have to repeat the process, sometimes two or three times.

Beach roses are used with early Nantucket postcards of island life on a painted wooden tray. The aqua color is reflected in a framed vertical wall hanging from a salvaged old quilt and a pitcher holding a single pink hydrangea blossom.

Wine Labels

On a trip to France we rented a barge with friends
to tour down the Canal du Midi. It was September,
which is grape-harvesting time. The fields along
the canal were brimming with grapes and farmers loading them onto carts for their ultimate
journey to be made into *vin du pays*. We drank the very ripe and not-so-good wine purchased
at every loch and always soaked the labels off the bottles to save for future projects.

Wine labels are especially interesting, and the designs are as varied as the product itself.
They can be quite attractive and good motifs for a découpage piece such as a serving tray.
When designing such a project, I usually arrange the labels so they overlap one another and
are placed at angles, often going up the inside edges of the tray as well.

OPPOSITE TOP

The grapes growing along the Canal du Midi in France during wine-harvesting season inspired the design for a tray.

OPPOSITE BOTTOM

For this tray I combined wine labels with a print of lush purple grapes (just like the real ones I saw on our barge trip). There wasn't enough material to fill in the blank areas around the labels, and the labels were too large to use more than two or three. Though I didn't have more grape leaves to fill in these areas, I did find green leaves from other prints to go with the color and shape of the grape leaves. This sort of grafting from one plant onto another is what makes the craft of découpage forever interesting as a creative medium.

BELOW

A round metal tray presents another version of a wine theme. Melissa and Dean Long own a local vineyard and make their own wine. The labels on their bottles are decorative and descriptive of the island, and the script lettering on each label, Nantucket Vineyard, is quite lovely and adds to the overall design of the tray. The ivory background of this tray complements perfectly the colors of the labels and grapes. The bottom of the tray is covered with purple marbleized paper to match the color of the grapes. On occasion, I paint the underside of a tray, using the same color paint I used for the rest of the tray. The bottom must be protected with at least three coats of sealer.

Tip: Soak the bottles in a basin of hot water to moisten the glue, and the label will slide off easily.

USES FOR SMALL TRAYS

A wooden or metal tray provides an interesting background for découpage and is an ideal accessory that is both decorative and practical. The flat surface is easy to work on, the confined area provides a perfect frame, and the design potential is limitless. I have designed many trays in all different shapes and sizes. I paint the wooden trays with water-based acrylic or latex paint, but for best results, a metal tray should be spray-painted with an oil-based enamel. The following are some uses for them:

- Trays are perfect for serving a small pot of tea, with a teacup and a plate of cookies.

- When serving coffee or tea to a group at your dining table, use a small tray to pass around the sugar, cream, lemon, and such.

- A decorative tray looks nice when placed on end on a shelf so the design can be seen. A small tray is easy to use as a backdrop with other three-dimensional objects such as a small vase of flowers, a figurine, or almost any collectible item.

- Arrange small items on the tray and place it on a coffee table or side table in the living room.

- Create a vignette on a small table that includes a tray and objects related to the theme. For example, if you've used floral cutouts, make an arrangement of the same cut flowers in a vase or floral pitcher. Add a few other items such as a lamp, a decorative dish, and a stack of botanical books.

For this project, I chose postcards with common colors and subject matter. Three lovely scenes of different beaches on the island suggested the theme for this tray. I began by sanding and then painting the tray in a pale seafoam color, suggestive of the ocean. Cutouts of shells and beach grasses add to the scene.

After first placing the postcards temporarily in position, I arranged the cut-out shells, some cut from wallpaper, others from wrapping paper, around the tray in obviously bare areas. Since the three paper elements I used for my cutouts are of different weight, each required a different number of layers of sealer to cover them sufficiently. For example, it took more coats of sealer to cover the thicker paper of the postcards than it did to sufficiently cover the thin wrapping paper cutouts. If you are a beginner, you should try to find designs that can be cut from the same paper.

PERSONALIZING
WITH A THEME

When choosing a theme for any project, begin by thinking about how the object will be used. Will it be displayed in your home? Consider the colors and patterns of the other elements in the room. If you have recently put up wallpaper, cut up the leftover pieces to make a coordinating accessory. When possible, I always recommend taking something—a color or subject matter—from your decorating scheme to use in a découpage project.

All sorts of early memorabilia are used to create a collage to fit each stair riser, designed by Richard Kemble. A clever way to tackle this project is to cut ⅛-inch pieces of plywood or masonite to fit the risers, découpage each one, and then attach them to the stairs.

Invitations and Announcements

Wedding invitations and birth or anniversary announcements can be preserved and incorporated into a découpage project beautifully. In this way, the event is memorialized. Boxes and plates of this nature are the biggest special-order items in my store. I like to think of them as future family heirlooms.

Illustrations on wedding invitations and birth announcements can dictate design motifs. The event itself is the most important indication of how these items should be designed, and the design of an announcement should indicate how one might go about choosing the cutouts to surround it. A birth announcement box, for example, should be soft and delicate, whereas a wedding plate might be more sophisticated than cute.

When working with any such material, I begin by trimming away the background paper, cutting as close to the printed announcement or invitation as possible. A paper cutter is best to ensure accurate straight cuts. Once the unnecessary paper is eliminated, the cutouts are arranged to overlap the cut edges and fill the top of the box or the back of the plate.

A wedding invitation surrounded by rose cutouts on a handmade box creates a future heirloom for the bride and groom, or their parents.

ABOVE

Gold paint is used for the background
of this plate made for a fiftieth
(golden) wedding anniversary
celebration. After trying several
different flower cutouts on the plate,
I settled on a print of deep purple
flowers. Purple represents a regal
theme and looks elegant against
the gold.

RIGHT

Delicate cutouts surround a wedding
invitation on a handmade box.

Mr. and Mrs. Charles Ross Carozza

request the honour of your presence

at the marriage of his daughter

Claudine

to

Thomas Nichols Biddison III

Saturday, the eighth of June

two thousand two

at two-thirty in the afternoon

Our Lady of Good Counsel Church

Secretary, Maryland

Wedding Plate

When I create a plate for newlyweds, I often ask what types of flowers will be chosen for the tables or what flowers will go into the bridal bouquet. In this way I can design the plate accordingly. I try to use larger flowers for these projects so that the design fills the area of the plate surrounding the invitation. I also try to find one print large enough to cut apart for the entire project. Then I don't have to combine different elements or search for several prints that work well together.

In general, when making a wedding plate, I cover the back with either paint or rice paper in a color to match the design. However, whether you use paint or paper, many coats of sealer are applied to create a strong, shiny finish on the back. When everything is dry, a band of gold is applied carefully with a brush, a gold pen, or gold leafing around the rim of my plates.

OPPOSITE
A contemporary wedding plate is designed with roses and daisies and backed with lavender rice paper.
RIGHT
For a golden wedding anniversary plate I tried many different flowers and colors before coming up with an appropriate design to complement the couple's original wedding invitation.

Baby Box

When designing a box with a birth announcement, I try a variety of cutouts to see which looks best with the design of the announcement. Sometimes I use babylike images. Other times I use delicate flowers. Another direction is incorporating whimsical images. The box is designed to create interactive play so the child can make up stories about what the children and animals are doing, what they are listening for, where they are going. *What does the pussycat say?* a parent might ask. *Where is the drum? Can you find the butterfly? The star? The yellow flower? What color is the boy's hair? What does the sheep say?*

ABOVE

For this box I tried yellow and brown sunflowers and yellow daffodils. I thought they might go well with the ivory-colored background, the gold embossed writing, and the simple image of the gold embossed baby carriage. However, it looked too somber. Next I tried larger cutouts, such as white narcissus, but the scale wasn't right for the project. After trying several different combinations, I settled on delicate, pale pink rosebuds.

RIGHT

The découpage images on this curved box were cut from a book titled *Nursery Friends from France*, copyright 1925. In this box I inserted a little poem that says "This little box is mine; I keep it all the time, to hold the things I treasure and things that give me pleasure."

The inside is lined with handmade rice paper in a color that matches the flower leaves and stems.

Note: Some wrapping paper is too thin and likely to wrinkle when glued to a surface. However, this shouldn't be a problem when the designs are tiny. Don't use too much glue.

5 PUTTING IT
ALL TOGETHER

Decorating with découpage can mean creating a vignette with a few frames on a table. It can mean reclaiming an old sideboard and turning it into the focal point in a room. Or decorating with découpage can be a way to add decorative touches that will transform a dull area into one that is charming and inviting.

Découpage is the way I add personality to a room with a handmade item. I work on anything from a tiny ring box to a large room-divider screen. The following houses were all decorated in different styles by homeowners who care about interior design. It was therefore a pleasure to see what I could contribute with projects that reflected the style of each home.

PREVIOUS SPREAD
The découpage bowl is decorated with coral roses on a dark green background. I always finish the edges of my glass pieces with a rim of gold leaf paint.

A HOME FOR
ALL SEASONS

Many homeowners collect and decorate their homes with items that reflect their area of the country. Here on Nantucket, homeowners collect and display marine artifacts, including lightship baskets. These baskets have a colorful history. Originally they were made in the 1800s by lighthouse keepers and sailors aboard whaling ships. Whether they are used as purses or to hold a bouquet of flowers, they are considered valuable collectibles not only on the island but throughout the world.

Peggy Kaufman is vice president of the Nantucket Lightship Basket Museum. She and her husband, Eli, are avid collectors of island artifacts, including a variety of baskets. It seemed fitting to use the Nantucket lightship basket as the theme for creating a group of découpage projects for their home.

Master Bedroom

The master bedroom is decorated in shades of blue and white, and this color scheme became the basis for my projects: a bed tray and night table to complement the pleated blue lampshades and collection of blue and white patchwork quilts. Blue and white is such a user-friendly color scheme that it's no wonder it is the most popular choice no matter where it's used in the country and no matter what new color is introduced each season.

Whenever I dream up a design and can't find the exact print or illustration that I want, I work with artist Barbara Van Winkelen. We have collaborated on many projects, including a special edition of Christmas plates. Together we talk about the floral designs I want, then she creates an original painting. In this case I commissioned a painting of a Nantucket lightship

basket holding a bouquet of blue hydrangeas. Barbara added the seashell and striped background. Originally I commissioned this painting for a line of fabric to make into pillows for my shop. We liked it so much that we not only used it for fabric but had prints made to cut out and découpage onto lampshades, trays, plates, and other accessories.

Basket of Hydrangeas Tray When designing the tray, I first had to make a copy of the print in a reduced size to fit the tray. Then I cut away the background, leaving only the basket of flowers and the shell. Once the tray was painted, I placed the design in the center and knew it needed something more. I glued real hydrangea petals, pressed and ready to use from the previous season, all around the basket so they looked as if they had fallen from the bouquet.For the bottom of the tray, I chose rice paper in a blue that matched the flowers.

Night Table This delicate table has nice proportions, and the height is perfect for holding a reading lamp next to the bed. I painted it white, then sanded lightly to rub away some of the finish, giving it a slightly distressed look.

As you can see, this print is larger than the one on the tray but not as large as the printed fabric used to make the pillow. By using one design in different sizes, you can create a coordinated look with your accessories that isn't too uniform.

After the print was cut out and glued to the surface of the table, I added a few pressed hydrangea blossoms to the "floor" area, as I did with the tray. Both objects are thus related in design and in placement of the elements. This pretty look reflects the interest of the homeowners.

Basket of Hydrangeas, a print by artist Barbara Van Winkelen, was the inspiration for the découpage accessories in this bedroom. The collection of early patchwork quilts, sheets, and lampshades creates a medley of blues. I added a few touches of yellow for zing. The pillow, night table, and tray are coordinated with the same design in different sizes. A small metal tin is spray-painted blue to match the colors in the room and découpaged with one hydrangea blossom. Real pressed hyrdrangea petals accent the tray. I love the combination of the real and cut-out designs on this project. If this is of interest to you, start drying flowers to press when they are in season and save them for your découpage projects. Since real flowers (even pressed) are thicker than cut-out paper, many more coats of sealer are required.

Kitchen

A Country Kitchen Two Ways The Kaufmans entertain often. Sometimes they have formal dinners in the dining room, but they are just as comfortable with six in the kitchen for homemade soup. I love their painted kitchen table and thought it would be fun to set it with two different themes, using my découpage plates.

Roosters and chickens are popular motifs in France. In Key West the roosters run wild and are both loved and despised. In Portugal it is a tradition to give something with a chicken or rooster motif to a new bride for her kitchen, and in Italy roosters are also a popular kitchen design. I find them a cheerful motif for many of my projects and have made hundreds of plates and platters with their images.

Blue and lavender hydrangea prints are used to create a lovely summer table setting. The centerpiece is a half-round tin planter with matching cutouts, and the large serving tray is also designed with the same prints.

To decorate an eating area in your kitchen, consider filling a country hutch with découpage plates, platters, and serving dishes all around a central theme. Each rooster and chicken print is slightly different, and I used the largest ones for the platters.

ABOVE

Roosters and chickens are used as the motif for a country table setting. The large plates are 9 inches in diameter and the smaller plates are 7 inches. See the following pages for the same table set in blue and white.

RIGHT

A 13-inch platter with rooster/hen motif.

Summertime Setting A pond, ducks, and a bevy of hydrangea bushes provide a peaceful scene just beyond the Kaufmans' kitchen window. Hydrangeas have become my design of choice for summer projects, so I couldn't resist a table with this theme. I combined plates with blue and lavender blossoms and different handmade papers for the backing in colors to match the flowers.

While poking around a local antique shop, I found two half-round flower containers made of tin. Tin can be painted with a brush or spray-painted, depending on where the object will be used. For outdoors, spray enamel is best. However, this project was created for indoor use, so I used latex paint in an ivory color. The découpage border around the tin is created in the same prints used on the plates and on the tray. I decided to line this piece in plastic to hold real flowers or small plants. Artificial blossoms can be used when the flowers aren't quite ready for picking.

IDEAS FOR A BLUE AND WHITE TABLE SETTING

- Use a mix of floral prints for the place mats and napkins.

- A blue and white plaid tablecloth will look good with the hydrangea theme as well. I use a patchwork quilt on my table.

- Tie blue grosgrain ribbon around each napkin and insert one hydrangea blossom.

- Decorate one corner of place setting cards with pressed hydrangea blossoms.

- A large basket of hydrangeas is a lovely centerpiece. Be sure to cut them low and arrange them tightly together so people can see over the top of the arrangement. Other containers you might use: a white pitcher, a blue-banded crock, a pail, or a champagne bucket.

- Though I use only white candles, blue ones would be just as pretty for this setting.

- For a Fourth of July setting, mix red tulips, white carnations, and blue hydrangeas.

- You can't overdo the blue color scheme when setting a table. Get out everything you own in blue and create an interesting scene down the middle of your table.

- Fill a basket with balls of blue and white yarn. Tie the handle with a wide blue plaid French ribbon.

- Fill bud vases with one blossom each and put one in front of each place setting.

Planter One day I received a package of wallpaper samples in the mail from a wall-covering company. One of the designs was a lovely yellow pattern that I decided to use on an oval-shaped planter for the end of Peggy's kitchen counter. Rather than paint the planter and arrange cutouts on it, I wrapped the tin completely with the wallpaper and then added the cut-out flowers.

I chose brilliant coral roses because the color looks so good on the soft yellow background. Many coats of sealer give this project a glossy finish and protect it from any spills when watering the plants inside.

Filled with two bright tulip plants, this container adds color to the end of the kitchen counter for a cheerful display, along with other potted plants. While we were photographing this project, Peggy's friend came in and declared the planter perfect for holding magazines in a guest bedroom. It is now residing in her house, proving that many items can serve dual purposes, depending on your needs. If you have an open mind, you might be able to solve a decorating problem in an unexpected way.

A strip of wallpaper covers this planter tin. Cutouts of orange roses and butterflies are applied over the wallpaper and protected with several coats of sealer.

The Living Room

A Rose Is a Rose Is a Rose The two pink upholstered chairs in the living room inspired me to use pink roses as a theme. I used the same table for the living room as I used in the bedroom, but with a different design. This is a good example of how an object can be designed in more than one way for different uses. I cut out one large print for the center of the table and saved a cluster of leaves to place on the front.

The lamp base was made of clear glass, and I used a smaller but similar rose print for this project. Découpage under glass is tricky, and placing it behind a curved surface is even trickier. However, with care it can be a very rewarding project, especially when making something to decorate your home. The blue-green paint creates a nice contrast and a soft pastel background for the rose print.

DESIGN FOR LIVING

If you're in a quandary about what items to découpage for your home, keep the following in mind: You know your own home better than anyone. You know what colors you like and how you like to use each room, what makes you feel comfortable, and when a little something is needed to complete a tabletop arrangement. When you live in an environment, you experience the feeling of the place—and that can be expressed in design. The objects and the cut-out découpage designs you choose will be integrated into the space and will work with the other elements.

Try this experiment. Lay out all the things you love to look at. Take one thing away. Keep doing this. Remove something; add something back until you have just three items that look good together. You'll begin to know just what is needed to complete a scene.

I used the same nicely proportioned table for the living room as that used for the bedroom. This time I designed it with a rose print to match the pink fabric on the chairs.

A TROPICAL PARADISE: THE KEY WEST INFLUENCE

Travel is a wonderful way to broaden your design outlook. Changing one's environment is exciting to a designer. It is easy to develop a style and then get stuck in that groove, but new visual experiences enable one to see new possibilities. Getting into another design mode can come from all different types of influences, from the area's natural vegetation, prevalent natural colors, lighting and climate, to building materials, architecture, and interior design styles.

Several years ago my husband and I collaborated on a book about the houses of Key West and fell in love with the island. Key West shares a similar history with Nantucket, although it bears no physical resemblance. In the tropical climate, plantings and the year-round outdoor living affect the interior design of homes.

The Key West style allows me to take a different slant with découpage designs and the projects I create. Colors appear more vivid in the South because the sun is so bright; this has a great effect

Tropical flowers and bright colors influence design in Key West. Living in a tropical environment means living outdoors more than inside. Doors are always open; therefore, the outdoors is part of any decorating scheme.

on the colors I choose when working there. We also have many artistic friends who live in lovely homes and we try to go on the annual house and garden tours for inspiration.

The plantings are lush and quite different from those in other parts of the country. Exotic plants and flowers and flowering bushes dominate the landscape. There is a passion there for orchids that rivals the New England hydrangea pride. Large leafy plants and hibiscus influence my sense of design, and I begin looking for objects to découpage with these cutouts. This year I brought big bright flower prints and citrus fruit illustrations with me, along with potential items to découpage such as trays, planters, and outdoor tables for holding drinks around the pool.

Pomegranates and tropical flowers are used to découpage small wooden tables for holding drinks by the pool. The tables are painted aqua blue and green to provide the background for the citrus.

A CONTEMPORARY HOME

Recently I designed some pieces to go with the decor in our friends' contemporary house. The owners, Richard Kemble and George Korn, have many talents. Richard is an artist, chef extraordinaire, and orchid enthusiast; George is the creative influence behind many local museum fund-raising events and an expert on the work of American artist Tony Sarg. Together, Kemble and Korn are dealers in American folk art, specializing in marine artifacts.

This house presented an interesting challenge because the owners are art collectors and the interior design is intended to complement and become an integral part of the art. Sculpture, folk art, and paintings mix well with found objects cleverly reinvented. The furnishings are mostly chrome, glass, slate, stone, and leather. This is not a home that cries out for vases filled with colorful flowers but rather a single white orchid. My usual country-style flower themes would not go with or enhance this environment.

Oversize planters, a large bowl, and garden and pool accessories seemed appropriate with designs borrowed from the vegetation surrounding the house and seen from inside. Large palm leaves and exotic flowers seemed most suitable here. I used Richard's orchids as the influence for setting a table on the deck with orchid plates. Large lemons provided another tropical design motif, so I made a few of these plates as well.

In a home that is designed in a mono-chromatic color scheme, brighter colors can be used on outdoor accent pieces. I used one large purple orchid in the center of 9-inch plates, then applied torn pieces of brightly colored tissue paper here and there on the back of the plates before backing them with white textured rice paper.

DECORATING TIPS FOR
A CONTEMPORARY LOOK

■ Accessories often look best when clustered together to make one definite statement. Much like a bouquet of wildflowers, bunching them together to make one dramatic scene has a greater impact than spreading them about like dots of color here and there.

■ One large object, such as an oversize bowl or lamp, in the center of a table or set off to one side becomes the focal point in the room, adding just one area of color.

■ A découpage planter for holding a single flowering plant, such as an orchid, on a pedestal against a white or pastel-colored wall is quite dramatic. Or you might découpage a pedestal to hold a vase of freshly cut flowers.

■ Choose one color or a single element to use for your découpage design: a large sunflower in the center of a table, for example, or a sunflower in the center of a charger plate. Look for prints to reflect the style of your home.

A wooden planter with orchid cutouts looks quite dramatic on a pedestal against a white wall and would be just as lovely on an outdoor bench by the pool.

Orchid Planters

I found two wooden boxes in an odd job lot discount store. The size and shape suggested their use as plant holders. I painted them leafy green and added a subtle sponge-painted texture to create a background that would blend with the environment.

I found several orchid prints many years ago, and now was the time to use them. If you collect interesting illustrations and images, eventually they will come in handy. Sometimes the print inspires a project; sometimes the object provides the inspiration.

The planters required two coats of green paint. Then I mixed a drop of black paint into the green for a slightly darker tone and used this to sponge-paint a texture over the painted surface. Once this was dry, I had a more interesting background over which to create a design. Orchids are graceful and elegant, and by wrapping the plant around the planter, I would be able to keep these characteristics intact. It takes a lot of cutting and rearranging of the elements in order to create an entirely new design that not only looks natural but conforms to the shape and size of the object.

Creating a Grouping

The coffee table is glass. The surrounding furniture is chrome and black leather. The wall expanse of French doors opens completely to the deck and pool, where the bright green foliage becomes the fourth wall. The tropical plantings provide the dominant colors in the living room, and I wanted to use them on three large objects grouped on the coffee table. I chose round objects, each a different size and height, to offset the angles of the furnishings and painted each dark brown with a subtle sponging of black to create the background for the bright tropical cutouts.

ABOVE
A round wooden bowl is designed with tropical cutouts to reflect the surroundings.

OPPOSITE
The lushness of the outdoors becomes part of this contemporary living room. The plantings influenced the direction for the découpage designs on the grouping arranged on the glass coffee table.

For the large, low bowl I used a variety of exotic flora around the inner rim. A large sunflower blossom proved to be the perfect color, shape, and size to anchor the design and, when placed in the bottom of the bowl, covered all the uneven stems of each element.

Since the design is so busy and colorful, I wanted a more subdued look for the small round bowl and tall curved vase—the supporting cast to the star of the show, so to speak. Aside from my lacking the right design elements, another problem became obvious. Working on a round or curved object is difficult with large paper cutouts. When glued around curves, paper wrinkles or creases at best. Sometimes you can cut notches at the edges, much like you would with a sewing project, but that can distort the printed design. This led me to another source: fabric.

ELEGANT CHARM

A home or a room can exude touches of elegance with just the right fabric or a small detail like a finely crafted piece of furniture. Elegant style is understated and unexpectedly comfortable.

Legendary fashion designer Pauline Trigère once said, "Elegance is confidence, chic is never doing anything by chance, and charm is an accident." Of course, she was talking about clothing style, but the same can be said about decorating a home. If one chooses wisely and knows how to mix the old with the new, creating different moods with confidence, the result can often be quite elegant.

Nancy Norris, an interior decorator, knows exactly how to design with elegance, charm, and comfort. Her Key West home in the lovely Casa Marina area fills the bill on all levels. Nancy divides her time between there and her home in Sun Valley, Idaho. We met in Florida

when her house was on one of the annual house and garden tours. This particular house was a rare treat, as it was furnished with the owner's exquisite collections from the Far East. The table settings alone filled my head with all sorts of ideas. Napkin rings, place mats, napkins, and plates were carefully chosen in rich Asian colors while dark brown lacquered baskets held exotic plantings as centerpieces.

Taking a tour through the first-floor rooms was rewarding enough. However, it was one of the second-floor bedrooms that made this particular tour especially worthwhile for me. The focal point of the room was the bed with a wonderful découpage frame created with cutouts from rose-printed fabric. The subdued yellow background of the bed frame was enhanced with a moss green silk coverlet

OPPOSITE AND ABOVE

This découpage bed frame, outlined with a bamboo trim, in Nancy Norris's granddaughter's room is an excellent example of fine workmanship and composition. The mustard yellow background has a painted crackle finish over which cut-out fabric roses and leaves were applied to create the elegant découpage design. Note how the design continues seamlessly from the side to the footboard with a concentrated pattern at the corners, leaving open areas so the design has breathing room. A close-up of the découpage reveals the precise cutting and detailed arrangement of the elements. More than thirty coats of sealer were used to cover the cutouts.

that perfectly matched the paint color in the room. The remarkable découpage work was done over a crackle-finish background. Upon close inspection, I realized there had to be more than thirty coats of sealer over the fabric in order to render it smooth to the touch. As a lifelong découpeur, I was incredibly impressed. "This is the Princess Room," Nancy told me. "I designed it for my granddaughter, and it makes her feel like a real princess when she's here."

Nancy found the bed for a client who changed her mind once it was delivered, which proved to be a good thing, because Nancy wished she had purchased it for herself. I especially like the bamboo frame and have filed this away for a future project. The trick is to find a plain and nicely shaped bed frame with découpage potential. This piece is a perfect example of the melding of elegant design and exquisite craftsmanship.

AN ARTIST'S HOME

My friend Maryann Gelula is an artist. Her home is minimally furnished because the rooms serve as a gallery for her artwork, which is forever rotating as her work is sold and new pieces emerge. The color scheme in her home is white with accents of earth tones, which are the shades of colors she uses in her work.

Several years ago I made a set of dessert plates for Maryann. Since her dining table is a honey-colored pine, she often sets the table with natural place mats and linen napkins. She requested that the background be a textured natural color with fruit motifs such as peaches, pears, apples, pineapple, oranges, and grapefruit. The plates look especially good on top of her

terra-cotta chargers, and I added a large
serving platter with a branch of peaches as the
découpage motif. A bouquet of coral-colored
tulips makes a perfect centerpiece for this
color scheme. The lace runner provides a
delicate contrast to the pine.

I have several prints of Indian corn that I use sparingly because it's a devil to cut the
wisps of corn hairs. However, I made two platters with them for Maryann. One has a neutral
paper background like the dessert plates and it looks sensational on a half-round marble
entryway table. The other looks completely different with gold marbleizing on a dark green
painted background. This plate is usually one of the accessories on her coffee table in the
living room. However, we tried it on top of a wooden cabinet in the dining room and liked
the way it designed with the grouping of photographs by her husband, Jerry. Adding two of
the dining chairs on each side of the cabinet seemed to complete that side of the room. On
the opposite wall are two of Maryann's paintings.

I designed a few other découpage pieces in keeping with the style of the house. Anything can be a starting point for a project. I especially like the elements on the fireplace mantel, which include one of my favorite paintings and Japanese lantern flowers. Their burnt orange color picks up similar shades of color found in the painting. Beside these things, there are three round objects: a barometer, a clock, and a tiny framed sailor's valentine made of shells. The tall, thin candlesticks lend height, and I wanted to add something round and golden for sparkle.

The gold frame was my inspiration, and I had no problem deciding to work on a round wooden charger plate that I spray-painted gold. But I agonized over the design until I found a print of a vine of squash with green leaves and zucchini flowers in an orange color much like the accents in the rest of the living room. The gold, the round shape, and the orange were just right to tie all the elements on the mantel together.

A vase similar to the one I designed for the Key West house (see page 105) seemed to have a life of its own. It looked good wherever it was placed. It is always amusing to find an object that looks as if it were made for the space no matter where it's placed. I set it in a niche in the bookcase, and it was right at home, adding a round

(see page 105)

OPPOSITE
A corn platter with gold marbleizing and hunter green painted background on a cabinet in the dining room. The corn picks up the colors of the bamboo dining chairs. A bowl of apples reflects the theme of the fruit plates on the dining room table.

ABOVE
The same corn print is applied with a neutral textured-paper background for a subtle look on a marble table. The colors on the corn platter are reflected in the painting by Maryann Gelula.

The mantelpiece in the living room holds a
combination of related items. The découpage charger
plate ties together all the colors found here and
throughout the house.

dimension inside the square cubicle. And again, when placed in Maryann's bathroom with the dark-wood countertop, this vase seemed meant for that space as well. I love to move things around from time to time when I get tired of an arrangement.

One of the very first pieces I made for the Gelulas' house was a 12-inch square telephone/ plant table. I used four old postcards of downtown Nantucket for the découpage elements and surrounded each one with rose cutouts just like the real ones that grow in profusion here all summer. This little accent table breaks up the stairway wall and is intended to hold one small element such as the tin planter I designed with cutouts of violets.

BELOW AND OPPOSITE
Sometimes an object looks good wherever it is placed. The round dark-wood vase decorated with deep red tropical flowers cut from fabric could be an artifact in the bathroom as well as the bookcase because it goes with the cherrywood surface and relates well to the two pieces of pottery in color, size, and texture, making an interesting grouping of like objects. Tall dried grass stalks or pussy willow would look good in this vase. (For a tropical look, see page 105.)

Small découpage accessories always add character to a coffee table, bookshelf, or occasional table without seeming overdone. Several years ago, when Jerry and Maryann's daughter Nicky got married, I made a wedding box for them with her invitation. This is one of the personal objects on the coffee table. Now there's two-year-old Ethan, so a grouping of picture frames seems in order. Each is painted pale yellow or green, and the flowers are lacy like those I used on the wedding box. Even when you add personal mementos and accessories to a room, design them within the style and color scheme you have established. A small wooden trinket box has a découpage design of orange and green flowers, and gold coasters on the coffee table are decorated with cut-out flowers to match the colors of the sofa pillows. Everything in this house is of a piece.

LEFT AND OPPOSITE
Nantucket postcards decorate the top of this 12-inch square plant table. The little tin holding rosebuds is an antique found in a folk art shop. It proved to be the perfect size for the violet découpage.

In keeping with the color scheme throughout the house, delicate flowers are used to découpage the pastel frames and round trinket box.

BELOW

Gold coasters are découpage projects made from round disks. The flower cutouts are in scale with those used on the wedding box. The soft decorations on these remembrance collectibles personalize the room.

GOLD COASTER

Thin wooden shapes can be found in a well-stocked craft store. You'll find round and square shapes, and ones like stars, animals, etc., that can be used for designing coasters. I used gold spray paint on all surfaces, top and bottom, then glued a circle of felt to the bottom of each coaster. Felt can be purchased in 9-by-11-inch squares that come with self-adhesive backing. However, nonstick felt can be adhered firmly with craft glue.

TIPS FOR DECORATING WITH NEUTRALS

- To keep a room looking streamlined and open, you need few colors and plenty of natural surfaces. Three shades of white, for example, can become soft and interesting with the introduction of natural textures.

- Floors that are varnished, bleached, painted, or pickled can be softened with seagrass mats, sisal, coir, or jute. If color is needed to make you feel more comfortable, consider kilims in earth-tone patterns.

- Tailored window treatments are best for a simple, streamlined interior. Wooden shutters, plain linen or bamboo shades, or unlined sheers work well.

- Add texture with natural baskets, wooden artifacts, ceramics, and natural fibers. Fresh flowers are important in a simple interior.

- The simple look can be expressed with an old distressed surface of a painted chair onto which you découpage a design with muted colors.

- Lighting is a key component. Overbright is harsh and unrelaxing; dimmer switches are a must.

The furnishings in the living room are white with accents of earth tones such as those found in the throw pillows and honey pine coffee table. The artist-homeowner uses the clean space to display her work in which she often uses these earthy colors.

A COLORFUL SETTING

Josine and Walt Hitchcock's home in the heart of Old Town Key West is just what you'd expect to find on this tropical island. Josine describes herself as an "all-around artist," and her house is a reflection of her creativity. Walt restores old houses, and he describes this house, where they live for half the year, as a labor of love. Bright colors abound, from the painted kitchen tables and chairs to the wicker sofas. Most of the furnishings were obtained from local yard sales, seconds shops, and literally off the street. Soft furnishings are covered with brightly patterned fabrics reminiscent of the south of France. It is a house decorated for casual living, and whimsy abounds. Josine and her artist daughter-in-law Karen have transformed all sorts of accessories such as vases, tables, chairs, and frames with their individual painting styles. When I saw the house, I knew it would be a lot of fun to create a few accessories to go with it.

I found an old wooden tray in a seconds shop. The paint was coming off in places, and there were slight chips and cracks here and there. The original painted roses were peeling and fading, but the graceful curves of the tray made it too good to pass up as a potential découpage project. After I smoothed out the imperfections with an electric sander, the tray was ready for three coats of gold spray paint. When in Florida, it's difficult not to look at oranges, limes, lemons, grapefruit, and kumquats as potential design elements. The oranges came from prints I found in Italy, and I envisioned them scattered over the tray. I like the idea of having fresh citrus out on a tray for a quick pickup.

Josine had painted a side table in a rainbow of colors, and the tray seemed a perfect accessory. The second tray was originally painted bright green. Again, a good sanding and spray coatings of gold transformed it into something worthy of a design suitable for the sun-filled living room.

This tray was a seconds-shop find. I sanded off the old finish and recoated it with gold spray paint. The fruit cutouts are scattered randomly over the surface for a diverse design. A project such as a tray that will be used often requires many coats of sealer to protect the découpage design. (Painted table by Josine Hitchcock. Painted lamp and peppermill by Karen Hitchcock.)

Gold Trays

I always look for used and new wooden and metal trays. At Christmastime I found square trays with lovely cut-out handles. This shape can be hard to find, so I bought four even though they were painted bright green with great big Santa Claus figures on them.

The trays were easy enough to sand. The old paint and the Christmas design came right off with the electric sander. I chose gold paint because it's a good background color for many flowers, especially shades of yellow, coral, green, and bright orange. Now and then I'll paint something a color I love at the moment without knowing what designs I will put on it. But then I have to search for the right cutouts or wait until I find something suitable. In a perfect world the object and design reveal themselves at the same time. While working on this book, I was partial to gold and celadon green. We design fabric for the shop, and one of the background colors we

If you find a tray that is already painted but you don't like the color, it is easy to repaint in the color of choice to go with your decor. The flowers were pieced together to fit the surface of the tray. Bright yellow, orange, and green look good against gold. The seafoam color of the green has been part of my repertoire for a long time, as it is a color interior decorators often use. It is easy to live with and creates a lovely background color for a floral motif. Butterflies make excellent accent spots when just a little bit more is needed.

One of the things to keep in mind when looking for items to découpage is how much preparation will be needed to make an object ready for the découpage process. If something simply needs to be repainted, it may not be a problem. However, if you have to first strip away an old finish before you begin, only you can assess how difficult this will be for you and whether the object is worth the trouble.

always use is celadon. I especially like to use it for large pieces of furniture, knowing it will work in almost any room decor.

The floral design for the tray was made with two identical prints. I needed one long flower and loved the colors of the tiger lilies against the gold. After cutting out the prints, I pieced them together to create one long flower with two blossoms and two leaves to fit the length of the tray. Then I found another lily that I positioned in the lower portion of the tray. I now had the two colors I wanted to dominate the design. The largest blossom on the right combines all the colors, but the shades are more brilliant and intense, adding a bit of punch to the overall design. I didn't have a stem for that blossom, but I did have a lovely, long-stemmed iris and was able to do a bit of grafting of one flower onto another. This is my poetic license and my flowers are rarely BC, "botanically correct." The head of the iris turned out to be just the right size, shape, and color to go with the other elements I used on the glass compote for Carol Fauth's house (see page 137).

Once the flowers were positioned and glued to the tray, I felt that the design was a little stiff. To create the illusion of motion, I added two butterflies, one alighting on a flower, the other in midair. Again, I used the color of the flowers. The bottom of the tray is finished with Florentine marbleized papers that I collected from trips abroad.Working with the papers I purchased in Italy brings me right back to that very spot and the experience of buying it. If you travel anywhere, look for something to make working on your découpage project extra special.

Three wooden saucers are painted burnt orange and découpaged with pressed flower prints I found in London. These flowers in similar colors are a good example of how you can use a design to fill an entire area or use a smaller cutout to leave more of the background showing all around. The nasturtium was the inspiration for these projects. Occasional items such as these can be used to add a spot of color wherever needed, and they come in handy for serving nuts or a round of cheese. They also make a nice trio hanging on the wall.

Flowering Planters

While the Hitchcocks' house is filled with color, the backyard is the epitome of a tropical setting. Beyond the deck, branches from the bougainvillea drip bright fuchsia blossoms, creating an idyllic, shady area for an afternoon repose. One of Josine's prized yard-sale finds is a dark green bistro table and chairs. One chair is seatless, waiting for Walt's attention. In typical Key West fashion it will be fixed "mañana."

Striped Planter

I filled one of my tin planters (see page 132) with a variety of flowering plants and plunked it down on one of the chairs just as the sun was streaking through the branches. It fit perfectly on the seatless chair, which may provide an alternative solution should the tropical torpor overcome the one in charge of repairing Josine's yard-sale finds.

The planter has a graceful oval shape with a scalloped edge. I painted it with alternating 2-inch-wide stripes of ivory and celedon green and then edged the rim with gold paint. I used a variety of materials to create the look of a border garden with lots of flowers growing at different heights around the tin. In this way I was able to use many of my leftovers.

A metal planter is painted with alternating stripes of ivory and green, then surrounded with a border of cut-out flowers. Note that the colors of the flowers are all similar in tone rather than soft pastels mixed with bright, intense shades.

My first idea was to keep the flowers within the stripes, but it didn't work out as planned, because the flowers simply didn't conform. Therefore, I ignored this constraint and placed the cutouts as if against a solid color background. Occasionally, an original plan can be altered and, as a result, improved as you go along.

When creating pieces to use outdoors, it is best to paint them with enamel and coat the cutouts with oil-base polyurethane. Read the labels on the cans of the materials to be sure they are meant for the surface on which you will be working. For example, there are paints that prevent rust on metal, or sealers to keep wood from rotting.

Note: All printed material will eventually fade when exposed to direct sunlight, no matter how many coats of sealer are applied on top.

Plant Caddy

An antique wire basket filled with "distressed" tins was irresistible as the basis for a découpage project. I love the challenge of cutting extremely fine material. The wooden handle cried out to be decorated with just this kind of cutout. The flowers I used on each tin have the same delicate proportions, but they're larger in scale, in keeping with the size of the tins.

The character of the distressed paint finish would have been destroyed if I had first painted each tin. Therefore, I was able to skip right to the design and finishing steps, eliminating the sanding and painting processes.

Accessories such as this add just the right touch of interest to any part of a home, whether indoors or out.

I added delicate cutouts to painted tins and the wire basket handle, then coated them with weather-resistant polyurethane. Note the tiniest of cutouts encircling the wooden handle and an even smaller cutout on the end of the handle. Save the tiniest buds in an envelope. They always come in handy.

A variety of metal containers in varying sizes and shapes suggest the découpage designs I used on each one. Long-stemmed white calla lilies work well on both the tall green bucket and the yellow pail, and the subtle pastel shades of celadon green, ivory, and butterscotch of the planters add just the right amount of color without detracting from the flowers and plants they hold.

OUTDOOR LIVING

ABOVE TOP
Sturdy workbenches made from discarded wood required a power sander to clean them up so they could be coated with a wood-penetrating stain.

ABOVE BOTTOM
Two coats of stain were required to bring the finish up to a rich cherry tone.

Carol and Gerry Fauth built their house in the historic area of Key West known as Truman Annex. Named after Harry Truman, this is where he vacationed during his presidency, and one of the tourist sites on the island is the house in which he stayed, called the Little White House.

The Fauths are no strangers to the island and consider Key West their second home for half the year. The rooms of the Bahamian-style house open onto a large deck that overlooks the free-form pool and adjoining guest cottage. Carol and Gerry are meticulous homeowners, paying careful attention to all the details that make their home an oasis in the heart of town. They travel often and pick up interesting pieces that add to their casual, comfortable style. The rooms are furnished with white wicker and Carol's favorite color scheme, blue and white with accents of bright pink. The deck, an extension of the living room, is decorated in a similar style. This is where the Fauths live and entertain in informal, Key West fashion.

Nothing was on the site when they built the house, and even the lush, tropical plantings that seem to have been there forever were their design. Pots filled with bright pink and white impatiens surround the pool and add a touch of color on the deck. Their home has been featured in many magazines, and it was hard to imagine creating anything that could add to this environment.

When I found a bunch of unrelated metal containers, it seemed fitting to turn them into planters using a variety of floral prints for the découpage. Carol has a great eye for detail and immediately saw them

grouped together on the wrought-iron plant holder that sits in an alcove by the pool. An interesting half-round window creates a crowning arch in the solid wall. When we later placed the yellow bucket on the deck, it was the perfect match for the little round iron plant stand. Grouping a bunch of planters together makes a dramatic statement. However, there is also the flexibility to move the individual planters around at will, in the sun or shade or wherever needed to add liveliness and color.

Decorated with flower cutouts, each bench can be used for drinks or plants by the pool or for occasional seating. I used a white metal bucket as the background for an orange daisy print and found just the right gerber daisy plant to fill the bucket.

    A few years ago Gerry made a couple of workbenches that had outlived their original utility. We thought they could be handy as occasional tables for holding a poolside drink, a plant, or, as Carol suggested, luggage in her guest rooms when needed. Though the wood was crude, the benches presented a wonderful challenge for a makeover. We used a power sander to remove all the dirt and crud that had accumulated. Two coats of cherry stain worked surprisingly well to create a sleek new background for the découpage designs.

The Fauths found a sweet little painting in the south of France and paired it with two Oriental figurines on a sideboard in the living room. The découpage bowl, though a new addition, has the flavor of the Orient.

It would be impossible not to use flower cutouts for an outdoor project, so I chose hydrangeas not only because the light colors looked so lovely against the dark background but also because they matched the color of the pool. For the other I used anemones in purple, pink, and red. I liked these darker colors even more against the stain.

I wasn't thinking of this house when I made the glass pedestal bowl. However, when I placed it on the sideboard in the living room between the two Oriental figures, it was as if it had been made just for that spot. The lavender iris and blue water lilies were applied to the outside of the bowl. I especially like the sinewy stems that gracefully conform to the shape. Once the bowl was dry, I spray-painted the outside with gold and then finished it with a bright purple tissue paper all over. The purple color shows through to the front as well, where the paint (intentionally) didn't completely coat the bowl. I used bits and pieces of blue paper over the purple, and with many coats of glossy finish, this project has the feel of the Orient, especially in this setting. The gutsy pedestal lamp and the cobalt blue vase holding white hydrangeas lend weight on either side of this delicate arrangement.

Yellow Flower Bucket

You can find painted metal buckets in all sizes and colors in many home centers or gift shops. A mustard yellow bucket seemed just the right color to go with the white lily prints I found during my teaching stint in Florence. I could imagine the finished project filled with white calla lilies or a white orchid. Sometimes it's a good idea to determine how a project will be used before making it. Then use dictates the design. I had the prints, but the trick was to make them conform to the curved shape of the bucket.

OPPOSITE
A perfect combination: white impatiens, white wicker, bright green palm fronds, and just that one subtle touch of yellow. Carol found the little round iron plant holder that turned out to be the perfect size to hold this container.

ABOVE
I cut the blossoms apart to design the flowers in such a way as to wrap them around the pail.

I cut out the prints and repositioned the elements so that I could use the whole design. I didn't want to lose half of it. If you start a project and in the middle find you don't have enough cutouts to fit the object, it can be difficult to find other motifs to go with the design. It's best to cut up what you have and make it work for you.

When the bucket was finished, one of Carol's white impatiens plants fit in it perfectly, and this project became a nice addition to the grouping, both in color and size. This object can also be used as a champagne bucket or for holding cut flowers on a table.

EVERYTHING'S COMING UP ROSES

Toby Greenburg renovated a traditional home on Nantucket. Toby has a sense of style and knows how to combine colors, a variety of prints, and different furniture styles to perfection. The accessories include books, framed family photographs, plates, needlepoint, and collectibles that once resided in her home in Baltimore. Her classic taste is reflected in the relaxed comfort, beauty, and warmth of the rooms, and I knew my room screen, with a predominantly rose design, would be right at home in this environment.

I have made several room screens, and each is entirely different. I like working on a large piece like this, which is similar to the screen I made for *Family Circle* magazine (page 176). However, this piece has a more complicated design and was therefore more difficult to découpage.

When you are working on a large project that requires many cutouts, it is always best to find the material from one source, if possible. The illustrations then design well together. The colors, the style, and the printing are integrated. The weight of the paper is the same throughout. I used the celadon green paint again because this color works well in a room with many other colors.

To differentiate the panel areas from the rest of the screen, we sponge-painted them with a mixture of equal parts glaze and the same paint to create a textured background.

A screen can be a focal point in a room. The rose theme is used throughout this room, combining prints on fabric, furniture, and accessories.

Sponging, ragging, and graining are decorative painting techniques that add interest to a surface (see Special Effects section on page 182).

When planning this project, I thought I'd use antique rose prints I'd been saving. I had just enough to fill each panel. However, after cutting one out, I was disappointed to find that it didn't look as dramatic as I had imagined and in fact was too small for the panel. I thought I could extend the stems and add some leaves to fill the area. I cut and prepared the necessary material and taped it in position on one panel. Right away I knew that the finished project wouldn't have the dynamic presence that it should have in the room. I reasoned that even if I had the prints enlarged, they would still be too delicate for the panels. Furthermore, the roses seemed too stiff for the potential offered by the graceful curve of the top. I needed to step back from the project until an idea came to me.

Our family was having Easter brunch at a local hotel when I noticed the printed tablecloth on our table.

TOP LEFT
A ready-to-finish screen is first sanded and sealed with two coats of sealer. It is then painted on both sides with two coats of celadon green.

CENTER LEFT
Different design directions are considered. The rose print proved to be too small and the fabric impractical.

BOTTOM LEFT
Equal parts of dark glaze and the background paint are mixed together for the sponging treatment. Experiment with different shades of color on a piece of poster board.

"This would be a pretty design on the screen. The flowers are large enough and the overall pattern flows nicely," I mentioned to Jon. "Why don't we look for just the right fabric and have it copied onto paper," he suggested. The next day we did just that. We bought several different pieces of decorator fabric in prints and colors that we thought would look good on the light green background.

We laid out the fabrics side by side on the worktable and traced various sections that I thought could be cut out to create a design for each panel. We then had two color prints made of each section. In this way I would have plenty of material from which to cut and piece together the design I had in mind. Cutting up the fabric itself was out of the question. I knew from past experience that the petals, stems, and leaves were too delicate to keep from fraying and the fabric too heavy to coat sufficiently with sealer. And if I needed more material, it would be more cost-efficient to make more prints than to buy more fabric. *Note:* This is an expensive way to get the designs you need, as we used several different decorator fabrics, and the cost of quality color printing is quite steep. You can certainly find less-expensive fabric with a lovely design. I mention this because cost may be a consideration before starting such a project.

TOP RIGHT
Using a natural sea sponge and rubber gloves, I sponged the glaze mixture over each panel for a subtle color and textural contrast with the frame of the screen.
CENTER RIGHT
Several different paper prints of the fabric were considered before cutting them all apart.
BOTTOM RIGHT
Masking tape holds different cutouts in place on the screen during the design process. Cutting up illustrations to re-create your own design is perhaps the most satisfying aspect of this craft. I move pieces from one area to another, cut apart, reorganize, and in general end up creating the finished design from scratch.

USES FOR A SCREEN

A room-divider screen is very versatile and can be used in a variety of ways, both practical and decorative.

- Create interest from above in a room where the rest of the furnishings are low.

- Use a screen in a corner of a room with a tall ceiling, for example, to make the room cozier.

- A decorative screen can hide a multitude of sins, such as an unsightly radiator.

- If you have an open kitchen, a screen can be most useful to block out the clutter when entertaining.

- Create a home office in a bedroom or corner of a living room and use a screen for privacy and to delineate the space.

- A screen is useful when you need storage space in a bedroom, for example. Hide extra blankets, a clothes rack, or an ugly but useful bureau.

- Finally, if you want to create a focal point in a room where none exists, a beautiful découpage screen could be just the ticket without a great deal of expense.

I spent the better part of a week cutting out all the designs I would need, taking care to cut even the half flowers at the edges and every small leaf or stem for possible inclusion. I thought I could use the original fabric to determine a logical arrangement of the cutouts, but it wasn't to be. For one thing, I was working on six panels that had to relate to one another as well as working with several different fabric designs.

After cutting the designs apart in logical places for convenient handling, I used masking tape to block out the layouts on the screen. My plan was to have the design flow from top to bottom diagonally across the panels. I was able to achieve this effect even though each panel is designed differently and I was using four different fabric prints. In the end I had to cut every bit of the designs apart and piece them together to conform to the plan. My final touches were applied with the leftover cutouts to the bottom of the screen.

For the large round glass bowl (see page 84), I used roses in shades of coral to go with those on the screen. The deep hunter green background enables the roses to pop out. I especially like Toby's window seat filled with pillows in a variety of different prints, including roses, plaids, and overall patterns. Here we see how so many different patterns, shades of color, and textures—wood, glass, fabric, mosaic, and brass—combine to create a stylish, eclectic environment.

I was very pleased with the finished piece, although I have to admit that my biggest problem was restraint. I kept seeing spots where I could add more. However, a good designer knows when to stop.

The black-and-white checker-board floor in the foyer creates excitement the minute you step through the front door. A green painted chair and antique mirrored cabinet against yellow-and-white-striped wallpaper offers an inviting vignette. A little 12-inch square découpage table fits nicely into this scene.

I had been saving a brown bird print left over from my china cabinet (see page 6). I liked its simplicity and graphic quality and used it on the top of the table. Since it looked too plain, I added a few green leaves to the top left corner for balance and to add natural color. The cutout of a nesting bird was just the right size to fit on the bottom shelf, and again I added a few green leaves to tie the top and bottom together and draw the eye down to this area. For one perfect accessory, I découpaged a square glass plate with a related design and used gold paint for the background. Nothing on this item detracts from the little area inside the front door; instead, something is added.

OPPOSITE
A black-and-white checkerboard floor in the foyer is bold and dramatic. The yellow-and-white-striped wallpaper provides a lovely background for a painted chair and delicate découpage table.
ABOVE
I used another bird print to découpage a square plate to just fit on the table. Gold spray paint provided the background, and I used bright red Oriental rice paper to match the flower for the backing.

6 THE DÉCOUPAGE PROCESS

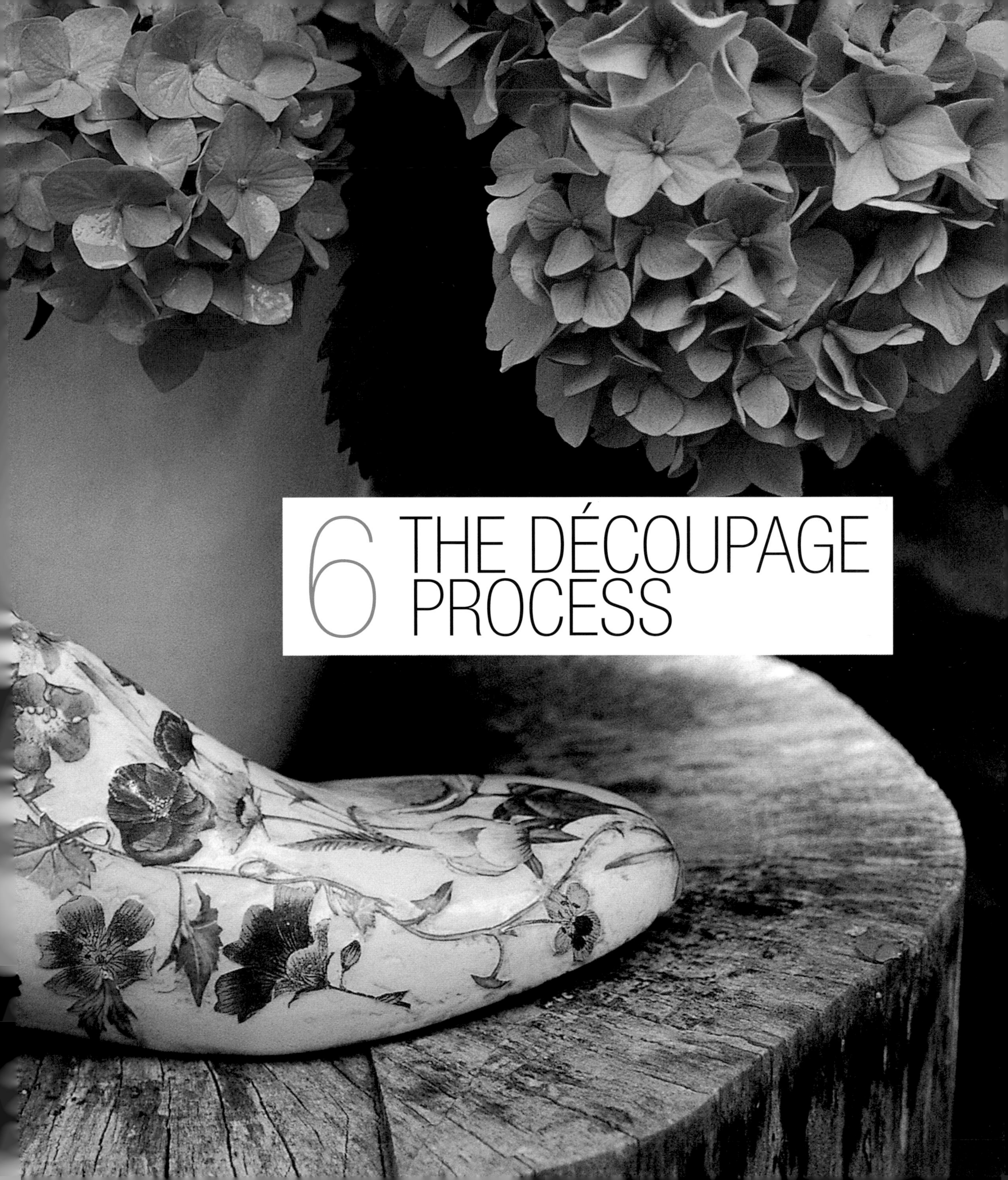

PREVIOUS SPREAD AND ABOVE
Antique wooden shoe lasts make an interesting
découpage project. In this case, I covered the
painted shoe last with lots of finely cut flowers.
OPPOSITE
Every year I make a series of découpage boxes
from my collection of prints of roses.

The technique of découpage can be used to transform unfinished furniture or refinish a painted or stained piece. Découpage can be applied on metal, wood, ceramic, or plastic, as well as under glass—inside a glass lamp, coaster, or vase, just to name a few items. You can even use découpage to recycle pieces that would normally end up in the garbage can. Never again will you throw away a plastic food container without first considering its potential as a beautiful découpage project.

The process begins when you find an object you want to work on and then the appropriate designs to cut out to apply to it. I can give you the step-by-step directions for technique, but it is the selection and arrangement of cut-out paper designs that make the end result an expression of your creativity. Getting a good eye for design takes a lot of practice, but it can be enormously satisfying.

MATERIALS NEEDED

The materials used for découpage are inexpensive and readily available. Craft stores are well stocked with everything you need, but you may have some of them in your home already.

Acrylic paint An unfinished wooden object (such as a plaque, box, or piece of furniture) should be painted or stained. I use acrylic paint for small items because it is available in small tubes in any color imaginable. Acrylic paint is readily available in art and craft stores. It is water-based, which means that your brush can be rinsed out in water and that the paint dries quickly, so you can apply two or three coats within twenty-four hours.

Latex paint This is regular indoor house paint that is water-based and therefore covers easily and dries to the touch in minutes. It cleans up with warm water. When working on large areas such as a piece of furniture or a section of a wall, I use latex paint. You can buy latex paint by the pint, quart, or gallon and have any color, picked from color chips at the paint store, specially mixed. If you have some latex paint left over from painting your walls, use it for a découpage project to display in that room.

Brushes You can use a natural-bristle brush or a foam brush for painting. Foam brushes are inexpensive and disposable. They can be cleaned with water and reused for both painting and varnishing or for applying water-based polyurethane. One sponge brush that costs less than a dollar can be used for an entire small découpage project. Découpaging a piece of furniture usually requires two or three brushes. Foam brushes come in different widths. Choose the one most suited to the size of the object.

I prefer a natural-bristle brush for most projects and use the same type for everything. Once in a while I use a sponge brush because it's right at hand. I keep coffee mugs to hold brushes of varying sizes in my work area. A natural-bristle brush lasts longer, through many projects if you clean it well with hot water. I find that using a bristle brush creates fewer air bubbles in the varnish; however, someone else working in the studio might find the sponge brush more effective. It's a matter of preference. Each brush needs to be the appropriate size for the project in order to get the best results. For example, a foam brush should be at least 1 inch wide for painting a small box, and a natural-bristle brush should be approximately $1/2$ inch for varnishing that same box.

Sandpaper Almost all wooden or metal surfaces must be prepared for the découpage process. Sanding the surface smooth is an essential step before applying paint or stain to the object you will découpage. It is also necessary to sand lightly between the coats of sealer that you apply over the cutouts on any surface, even the back of glass.

I have always used 3M WetorDry black flint paper, which is available in all hardware stores. You'll need at least two or three sheets each of #400 and #600 grit for fine sanding. If you are doing découpage on an old piece of wooden furniture, you'll need a medium #80–100 grit sandpaper as well. This sandpaper removes any finish that was previously applied. A thorough sanding takes off the old finish so you can apply a fresh coat of paint. If you intend to stain the piece, you'll need to remove the old finish completely, which might require a strong stripping material as well as an electric sander.

Sand metal lightly with the fine #400 sandpaper to enable the paint to adhere to the surface.

Varnish A water-based, fast-drying, nonyellowing varnish is one kind of sealer for découpage. Varnish comes in different finishes: satin (sometimes called matte), semigloss, and glossy. The finish is a matter of preference. I usually use a satin finish on most of my projects. Occasionally I choose a glossy varnish for the back of my plates when I want a shiny finish.

Varnish comes in many sizes, from a 2-ounce jar to a gallon. For most découpage projects, a pint is sufficient. Most découpage projects require from five to twenty coats of varnish to cover the prints, depending on the thickness of the paper cutouts. The object is to create a buildup of coating over the cut-out designs so they are smooth to the touch.

Polyurethane This sealer is similar to varnish, but some think it provides a stronger finish. Oil-based polyurethane can be used on outdoor projects such as a mailbox or patio furniture. Water-based polyurethane comes in satin, semigloss, and glossy finishes as well.

Acrylic medium Also called acrylic polymer, this water-based medium looks like milky white glue but dries clear. One of its attributes is that it can be used to glue down your cutouts as well as coat and seal the surface of your découpage project. It dries hard and fast, which means you can apply several coats (and thus finish a project) in one day.

Designs There is an enormous amount of printed material available for a découpage design. The quickest and easiest source is a card shop, where you'll find a variety of wrapping paper, greeting cards, stickers, and calendars. You can also use postcards, posters, photographs, wallpaper, valentines, and such memorabilia as ticket stubs, napkins, and invitations, as well as fine prints, books, and other illustrations. In other words, almost anything that is printed on paper.

The first question people ask me is "What about magazines?" I don't encourage using magazines for a few reasons: the paper is thin and often wrinkles when glued to a surface, sometimes the printing ink smears when varnish is applied over the printed designs, and often the printing shows through from the underside. However, if you do use a magazine cutout, test the sealer on the paper before applying the cutout to the object on which you are working.

Scissors I use cuticle scissors almost exclusively. The curved, pointed blade enables me to cut delicate flowers, fine stems, and jagged-edged leaves. I use the point to get into difficult-to-reach areas between flower petals. Embroidery scissors are an alternative, and sharp, straight sewing scissors are fine for cutting a large poster or print. I use these scissors to trim around the outsides of prints where there is a lot of white space to remove, but my sharp, fine cuticle scissors are always by my side—the finer the blade, the better. I prefer stainless-steel scissors that cost about fifty dollars. I keep this pair in an area where I do most of my cutting. However, I also use inexpensive scissors from Revlon because I have many pairs all over the studio, in my purse, at the store, and everywhere else that I do any cutting. Always clean and sharpen scissors between projects.

TIP: You can easily sharpen scissors by using them to cut up pieces of sandpaper. Never ever use your découpage scissors to cut anything but paper if you want them to last for a long time.

Glue After the paper designs are cut out, they are applied to a surface with glue. I prefer white craft glue for every project, whether I'm working on wood, metal, plastic, or glass. Occasionally I use the acrylic medium for my glass projects.

Sponge A regular kitchen sponge is indispensable for découpage. It should be clean and damp when used to press down on the cutouts once they are glued. A sponge is also needed to wipe away excess glue that invariably seeps out from the edges of the cutouts once they are glued down securely. You can cut a large sponge in half for a more manageable size.

Wax Once I've applied the last coat of sealer and sanded the surface smooth, I add a coat of clear furniture paste wax to protect the finish, no matter what surface is under the sealer. I have been using the same can of Butcher's Bowling Alley Wax for more than twenty years because only a very thin coating is needed on a finished découpage piece. Other fine brands are Johnson's and Goddard. You'll find furniture paste wax in supermarkets and hardware stores.

Soft rag and paper toweling A soft rag is essential for wiping the piece clean after sanding as well as for buffing the wax on a finished project. I use a terry-cloth rag and, when I have one, an old T-shirt or cloth diaper (almost nonexistent). Paper toweling is a must when you're working on any craft project. Use it for wiping up spilled paint, glue, varnish, or stain, as well as a rag substitute if necessary for buffing the wax to a fine sheen on a finished project.

Sheets of plastic or drop cloth The worktables in my studio are counter-height because I work standing up. Each table is covered with kraft paper when I paint. I then cover the paper with easily removable sheets of heavy plastic for the gluing process. When I lift each cutout, it won't stick; and when I'm finished gluing, I can easily wipe the plastic clean with a sponge and hot water. A canvas or plastic painter's drop cloth, sold in hardware stores, is excellent for covering a worktable.

Antiquing (optional) I left this item for last, as it is an optional process. For more than twenty years I used an antiquing solution to add character to my finished boxes. I like the aged look, especially on a box that looks as if it were already an antique. The boxes that my grandfather made had that quality and when finished looked too new without some sort of "dirt" indicating that it had been around for some time, perhaps an heirloom recently recovered from someone's attic. However, once I had a store and was exposed to the people buying my work (as opposed to selling it to another store that would then sell it to a faceless customer), I began to get feedback. "This piece is dirty," they would say. "Can you clean it up?" I have since stopped antiquing all but my really old-looking boxes that my grandfather made. I use them sparingly, even though he left me a wonderful legacy of many handmade boxes.

If you want to make a project look old, you can do so with a premixed antique solution found in most art or craft shops or you can use a small tube of raw umber to create your own. (See "Antiquing," page 182.)

HOW TO DO DÉCOUPAGE

Wood has always been the best surface for découpage and is the one on which I learned the craft. It is the most traditional surface for découpage. You'll find a variety of boxes, plaques, small pieces of furniture, trays, frames, light-switch plates, napkin rings, tissue holders, and other such items in most hobby shops or unfinished-furniture stores. Look for unusual items at yard sales, seconds shops, junk and antique stores, auctions, and even in your own attic or basement. An old marred or chipped item can be reclaimed for a découpage project that might turn out to be the most beautiful object in your home.

1. Sand the item you have chosen to découpage.

Pine, birch, maple, and oak are just a few of the woods used to make furniture or craft items for decorative finishing. Unfinished pieces are fairly smooth, requiring very little sanding. An old piece of furniture needs to be sanded before giving it a coat of paint. Always sand with the grain of the wood, not across it.

The goal is to start with a smooth surface. Each subsequent step along the way will then be the best it can be. Begin by sanding the object several times. When sanding between coats of paint, use #400 sandpaper. After applying the cutouts and the sealer, lightly sand each coat of sealer with #600 sandpaper.

2. Apply the base color.

It doesn't matter whether you use a foam or natural-bristle brush, the technique of painting is the same. Always apply the paint in one direction and then lightly brush the opposite way. For a textured finish use the sponging technique (instructions on page 183). Be sure to cover all areas.

When working on a box with hinges, it isn't necessary to remove them. You can easily paint around them with a pointed artist's brush. Another option is to paint right over the hinges. Most manufactured boxes are made with stapled hinges, unlike those found on an antique box, and they actually look better when painted the same color as the box. However, if you don't like this idea, carefully paint around the hinges and remove any paint that gets on them with a single-edged razor blade once the paint is dry.

If a project needs more than one coat of paint, let the first coat dry thoroughly before applying a second one. This usually takes at least two hours. If brushstrokes are visible in the dry paint, sand lightly with fine #400 sandpaper to make the painted surface smooth.

3. Cut out the design.

When you are cutting out illustrations, the goal is to cut away as much of the excess background paper as possible. Even if the paint on an object is white and you're cutting away white paper, if you leave any of the paper between the flowers, for example, it will not look the same as if it were cut away. You will not have the same definition around each element.

If a cutout is too large to fit onto an object, it can be cut apart and altered to fit. The cutout doesn't have to be used exactly as is.

Fine Cutting When cutting very fine motifs, you need sharp, finely pointed scissors. I use stainless-steel cuticle scissors with a curved blade, which allow me to get into small areas. By holding the scissors with the curve outward, I don't run the risk of cutting off a stem or leaf by accident. If this happens, you can always glue the pieces of a cutout in place on the object where needed. It is most unlikely that you'll find a perfect design to cut out in the exact size to fit the object on which you want to apply it. You can lengthen stems and add leaves or buds to flower stalks. This is how you create a design that looks best. This is the part of découpage that makes the craft interesting, exciting, and stimulating.

4. Arrange the cut pieces into a design.

I begin the design process by loosely arranging the cutouts on the object. Then I rearrange them until I'm pleased with the way the design looks. When working on a three-dimensional object, such as a box, I treat it as a whole, rather than designing each side and top as a separate entity. I strive to make the design flow from one side to the other, from top to front and from front around to the sides and back. In this way the overall effect is more interesting than static.

If the project is a flat object such as a plaque, tray, or the top of a small night table, the design challenges are different. Essentially what I have is a blank canvas on which to create a "painting." However, here, too, I have to decide whether to place one cutout in the center, create a border, put one element in each corner, etc. It's important to take time with this part of the découpage process. You want it to look as good as possible. The technique may be flawless, but if the design isn't the best you can make it, you won't be happy with the end result. Sometimes I let a layout sit for weeks before I go back to it with a fresh eye.

5. Glue the design in place.

Once the designs are arranged on the painted or stained surface, remove each cutout, one by one, and place it facedown on your work surface. Because I cover my worktable with a sheet of plastic when gluing, the cutout won't stick when I lift it up. Other options for a gluing surface are a pane of glass or a ceramic tile. Squirt a small amount of glue in the center of the back of a cutout and spread it evenly to all the outer edges. Position the cutout on the object and press it down with a slightly damp sponge. Remove any excess glue from around the edges. Press the cutout down again with a damp sponge and then a dry cloth or paper towel.

Continue to apply all paper cutouts in this way. Let the glue dry for at least an hour for small cutouts, overnight if it is a large solid print, invitation, photograph, poster, or postcard, for example.

6. Seal the design.

When applying the sealer of choice, whether it's varnish, polyurethane, or acrylic medium, always work in only one direction. Apply a thin coat of sealer across the entire front of the object. Continue to coat all exposed areas of the object. Without adding any more sealer to the brush, drag it lightly across each coated section in the other direction. Since the sealer is clear, if it's applied against the light, it's easy to see any areas that have been missed. Let the sealer dry thoroughly according to the directions on the can or bottle.

I apply at least two or three coats before sanding lightly over the dry finish with #400 or #600 sandpaper. Then wipe the object clean. More coats of sealer are added as needed. I am never satisfied with the finish until at least ten coats have been applied. To determine how many coats of sealer your project needs, run your fingers over the finish. If the edges of the cutouts feel smooth (the design will be slightly raised), enough sealer is covering the cutouts to protect them. If not, apply another coat or two. I often apply twenty to thirty coats of varnish or polyurethane (they are interchangeable) to a tray, table, or anything that will get a lot of use. I also apply that many coats of finish over fabric or postcards, wedding invitations, collage items such as ticket stubs, and any paper that is thicker than a sheet of bond paper.

Sand the final coat of sealer unless you are planning to apply an antique mixture to the finish (see page 182). Wipe the piece clean with a damp sponge and then a paper towel.

7. Preserve the project.

To preserve my finished projects and give them a lustrous sheen, I use a soft cloth or paper towel to coat the entire piece with a light film of furniture paste wax. This dries in minutes. I then use a clean cloth to buff the finish to a lovely, soft sheen. This protects the object from wear and tear. Just as you might treat your furniture, applying wax to a découpage piece twice a year or whenever the finish becomes dull-looking will keep it looking beautiful.

TECHNIQUES

Découpage on Furniture

A painted red sideboard decorated with découpage is reminiscent of Chinese lacquered furniture. It can serve as a focal point around which to build a room. I retrieved this piece of furniture from the junk heap, stripped and repainted it, then découpaged the front with cut flowers and butterflies for use on a protected porch. The contrast between the elegant and rustic appeals to me. At other times it has served as a buffet table in my dining room.

There are many different shades of red. Some lean toward the pink red of brick or terra-cotta, others have blue or purple in the color. Then there are the clarets. Each shade creates a different atmosphere. Dark cranberry red is often found in early New England houses. Used with deep green or Federal blue, you have a perfect early American mix.

TOP RIGHT
The sideboard is first stripped of its finish.
CENTER RIGHT
Two coats of red semigloss latex paint are then applied.
BOTTOM RIGHT
Paper illustrations are cut out with very fine cuticle scissors.

ABOVE

The cutouts are arranged in a pleasing way and glued to the background.

ABOVE RIGHT

Many coats of sealer are applied to the entire piece to give it a smooth, satin finish.

When painting a large piece of furniture such as this, add glaze to the paint to give it a bright, rich finish. Sometimes deep red, right out of the can, appears muddy and dull after it dries. If so, apply a coat of semigloss clear polyurethane or varnish (non-yellowing) for the glazed effect. Then you're ready to apply any découpage design.

Découpage under Glass

A variation of découpage is crafting under glass, which is called "reverse découpage" because you apply glue to the front (not the back) of the cutouts, which are then placed under the glass item. Reverse découpage is often used to decorate the inside of glass lamps, which is how it was done when the craft originated many years ago. Once the design is applied to the underside of glass, apply the paint over the back of the cutout under the glass. No sealer is necessary for a vase or lamp, but work under a glass plate must be sealed.

I make hundreds of glass plates every year for my store. I first introduced them with a demonstration on *Oprah,* and they have become quite popular, as they are decorative but can also be used for serving food.

Making a Découpage Plate   Start with a clear glass plate. Be sure to clean and dry it thoroughly. You'll also need a damp sponge; white craft glue, such as Elmer's Glue-All, or acrylic medium; a cut-out image; a bowl of warm water; and a dry cloth.

1   Place the design in the water to soak until it is saturated and uncurls.

2   Coat the back of the plate generously with the glue or acrylic medium.

3   Pick up the cutout and carefully place it, facedown, on the coated back of the plate. Don't worry about the white film of glue over the cutout.

4   Press the cutout down on the underside of the plate with a damp sponge while carefully patting away any excess glue or acrylic medium. *Note:* Do not rub, pat.

5   Turn the plate over so you are looking at the front and gently press over the image from the underside with your fingertips to distribute the adhesive. Keep pressing from the center outward to remove all air bubbles. I use a burnishing tool, which is a soft plastic item about the size and thickness of a credit card, to adhere the design and press out air bubbles. However, this tool (available in art stores) can rip the paper if you apply too

much pressure. I recommend it only after much experience with adjusting the amount of pressure needed. Pat away the excess glue once more with the damp sponge.

6   Turn the plate facedown and let it dry overnight. Any adhesive film left on the plate or the image will dry clear.

7   I used handmade paper to back Maryann's plates (page 108–9), but there are alternatives: wrapping paper, napkins, tissue, or paint. Each provides a different texture and finished look.

8   Use the plate as a guide to draw around the paper and cut out one piece.

9   Apply the same adhesive used to adhere the motif and spread it generously over the front of the paper and back of the plate. Place the wet paper over the back of the plate. Don't worry if there is overlap at the edges. Smooth the paper down with your hands and press out the air bubbles.

10 Let the plate dry overnight. Trim excess paper from around the plate rim with a brand-new single-edge razor blade. The paper must be completely dry before doing so, or it will rip unevenly and pull away from the plate.

11 To finish and protect the plate so it can be used and washed by hand, apply several coats of clear sealer to the back. Each coat must dry for several hours. If the plate is being made for decorative purposes only, cut a piece of felt the size of the base and glue it to the back.

12 When the plate is complete, I add a rim of gold paint around the back and front edge. This can be done with an indelible gold pen or gold leafing paint. It takes a steady hand to apply it smoothly all around. If, for example, you slip and get paint on the plate, let it dry and then scrap away the mistake with a razor blade.

RIGHT

Coat the front of the print and back of the plate with adhesive and fuse them together.

BELOW

Once everything has dried, apply colorful paper to the back of the plate with sealer or craft glue. The white film will dry to a clear finish. Coat the back with sealer.

How to Line Anything with Paper

The following directions apply to lining anything, small or large, including dresser drawers, boxes, or trays:

1   Measure the left and right side of the inside of the object.

2   Measure the front, bottom, and back inside surface to cut as one continuous piece.

3   Even when a box is uneven, use a ruler or straightedge to mark the measured lines on the back of the paper. Add a little extra when cutting out the pieces so they can overlap to the front, back, and bottom of the drawer. In this way, when you glue down the larger piece, there will be no uncovered space where the papers meet at the inside edges.

4   Coat the back of each piece of paper for the sides with glue, making sure to get the outer edges all around. Place the paper inside each side of the item and smooth it down. It is helpful to use a blunt object such as a butter knife to secure the paper into the corners. Wipe away any excess glue that may seep out of the edges.

5   Next, spread glue over the back of the largest piece of paper and with the box, for example, in front of you, line up one short edge of the paper with the inside front edge of the box. Press down and continue to smooth the paper into position inside the box. Take care to press the paper into the bottom of the box and then bring it up to finish the inside of the back wall, which is now facing you. Use a sponge to pat and smooth the paper down securely.

6   Once the item is lined, let it dry overnight. If a little bit of paper extends over the top of the rim, wait until it is dry, then trim it with a sharp razor blade. *Note:* Do not trim before the paper is dry, or it will pull and rip unevenly.

7   Once the paper liner dries, apply two or three coats of sealer to protect it.

8   Measure and cut a piece of the matching paper to fit the outside bottom of the box. Spread glue over the bottom of the box or on the back of the paper and place it in position. Press and smooth it down to remove any wrinkles or air bubbles.

9   If you are working on a tray or anything larger, use a wet sponge brush to spread the glue, diluting it slightly. After placing the paper on the bottom of the tray, smooth and press it down firmly to remove wrinkles and air bubbles. A wallpaper brush or roller helps with this process. Be careful not to rub it too aggressively with a wet sponge, or the paper will tear.

10   Let it dry. Then apply two or three coats of sealer for protection. Allow each coat to dry thoroughly before applying the next one.

CHOOSING PAPER

Many art stores carry all sorts of decorative art paper that will add a professional-looking finish to your project. Use art paper for lining boxes and covering the back of découpage plates. One paper in particular is quite popular, a Thai paper called mulberry. Mulberry is an Asian shrub called kozo. This paper tears easily and adheres well and produces an interesting finish. It comes in a multitude of colors and, unlike Japanese kozo, is reasonably priced.

European papers, originally made by hand centuries ago, are now being mold-made and are available commercially. You can find a wide variety of handmade papers at most art stores or upscale card shops.

Although paper comes in many weights, it generally falls into three categories: light, medium, and heavy. The medium-to-heavy-weight papers are generally of handmade European stock and cost more than machine-made papers. These are all acid-free.

Japanese papers are medium-weight for the most part and are used in fine art and decorative projects. The variety of colors and textures is unbeatable. You can choose a color to match the front of a box, or in the case of plates, the color and texture of the paper will determine the look of the front of the plate.

Découpage with Fabric

Fabric is an excellent source for découpage designs. However, fabric that is too thick, such as upholstery weight, is difficult to cover with fewer than thirty or more coats of sealer. If the material is too thin, the edges will fray when you cut it. Delicate prints are similarly difficult to cut. There is a product available in fabric stores to apply to the fabric before cutting to keep it from fraying, but this solves only one problem and I don't find it 100 percent foolproof.

The good news about fabric is that it can be copied onto paper. Consequently, you have many choices; most fabric prints come in several colors, so if you find a design you like but the color isn't right, there's a good chance you'll be able to order the same print in a color to go with your room. When is fabric a good choice for a découpage project? When you're working on something that is curved or round, and the material has to give. Then you need the flexibility that can come only from a fabric cutout.

Applying Fabric Cutouts

When creating a design with fabric cutouts, the object on which it will be placed must be coated heavily with white craft glue or acrylic medium. You can do this with your hands or a wet sponge brush. Then dampen the cut-out fabric slightly by pressing a wet sponge over it and lay the fabric piece in position on the

A tall vase is designed with fabric cutouts. This découpage project on a plant stand fills a corner of the room, adding interest at the foot of a staircase.

glue-covered object. Press over the fabric with your hands, molding it to the shape as you do so. Use a sponge to pat the fabric down until it is completely smooth and glued to the item. Remove any excess glue or acrylic medium with a wet sponge, then pat the design all over with a dry cloth.

Finishing Allow the applied fabric to dry thoroughly overnight. Then begin the sealing process. Brush the sealer of your choice over the entire object and let it dry. It takes sealer longer to dry over fabric than over paper. Continue to apply as many coats of sealer as it takes to completely cover the fabric cutouts and render the object smooth to the touch.

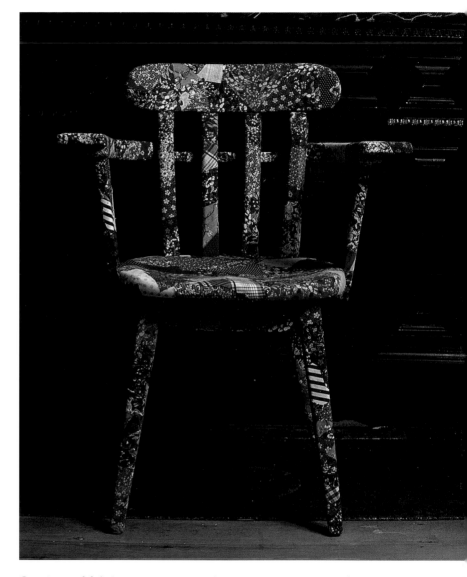

Cut pieces of fabric remnants are used to cover every square inch of this chair. Many coats of sealer protect the fabric cutouts and give the chair a glossy finish. Regular craft glue was used to attach the fabric.

Découpage with Wallpaper

Wallpaper presents interesting possibilities for design motifs. It is an excellent source of material when you are working on a large object such as a piece of furniture. If you are wallpapering a room, be sure to save some leftover pieces to cut up for découpage accessories in the room. A wallpaper border is another source for a design, such as that used on the farm table shown on page 26.

Applying a Wallpaper Border to Furniture

Whether applying prepasted or regular wallpaper to furniture, I always coat the back of the design liberally with white craft glue.

1   Measure and cut each strip of wallpaper border.

2   The corners can be mitered or can butt where they meet. If mitering the corners, cut each strip of paper to the exact measurements of the table.

3   To miter the corners, place each strip down on all sides. The corner areas will overlap.

4   Place a straightedge ruler over the paper strips, on the diagonal from the point of the corner of the table.

5   Using a razor blade, slice through both layers of paper. Discard the excess, overlapping pieces.

6   When gluing each strip in place, be sure to butt the cut miters together evenly. To butt ends together, simply measure and cut the long pieces first. Glue them in position on the tabletop. Next, cut the shorter end pieces and glue them in position in the same way.

7   Let the wallpaper dry overnight before coating it with sealer.

If you collect pottery or sculpture, display it on a découpage pedestal. Plain wooden pedestals were made with finished plywood, painted, and decorated with wallpaper cutouts.

A Wallpaper Project

I like to work on a large piece of furniture that will make a statement in a room. Several years ago I made a wooden room-divider screen for a *Family Circle* magazine project. Even though the screen is large, I designed it as a very easy découpage project that anyone could do. The screen was made of ready-to-finish pine and consisted of three large panels hinged together. Each panel was divided into four sections. When working on unfinished furniture, begin by sanding the entire piece and then wiping it clean. This is a necessary step before painting or staining the wood.

Once the paint was dry, I outlined each section of a panel with a darker shade of the background color to create a frame around the planned découpage design. I found a pretty wallpaper pattern and cut out squares to fit each panel. Once the cutouts were glued in place, several coats of clear sealer were applied to the panels. To finish this design, I glued embroidered ribbon between each panel and topped each curved section with a bow. (For another version of a room-divider screen, see page 141.)

LEFT
A blanket chest is covered with many diamond-cut wallpaper pieces to create a quilt pattern. Several coats of sealer protect the finished piece.

OPPOSITE
Dress up a guest room with a valance covered with a pretty wallpaper border. Use the same wallpaper to cut out the design to découpage a simple painted dresser.

OPPOSITE

Each panel of this room-divider screen is covered with wallpaper. Embroidered ribbons add a finishing touch.

TOP LEFT

A ready-to-finish toy chest was painted pale blue, then decorated with a strip of wallpaper. I also used the paper to cut out enough daffodils to create a border along the top. More of the paper was used for the stool and bucket.

BOTTOM LEFT

Wallpaper with a whimsical barnyard motif was used to découpage a painted school chair.

Découpage with Pressed Flowers

Pressing flowers is a passion of mine. When my garden is in full bloom, I have California poppies, bright blue hydrangea bushes, tulips, roses, and a variety of other flowers. I often press the petals and leaves to use in my work. Whenever I go on a trip, I pick and press a flower from the area I'm visiting and preserve it, along with my notes in my travel diary.

Pressed flowers offer wonderful design possibilities for a découpage project. Flowers that press well include black-eyed Susan, cosmos, daisy, heather, poppy, lavender, Queen Anne's lace, tansy, buttercup, and zinnia. It is easiest to press naturally flat flowers such as a pansy, but don't limit yourself to them. In my experience, buttercups have proved to be the best flowers for pressing and using in a collage, for flower arrangements under glass, or for découpage.

Poppy petals, pressed in a thick book to dry, have become translucent.

When handled carefully, they are quite easy to work with. Best of all, they retain their color.

How to Press Flowers

1   Begin by cutting up white blotting paper or paper toweling into pieces approximately 8 x 11 inches.

2   Cut corrugated boxes (found in supermarkets) into pieces the same size as the pieces of blotting paper. It's easy to cut boxes up with a single-edge razor blade or craft knife.

3   Place several flowers and leaves on a piece of blotting paper or toweling so the flowers don't overlap one another. Each page can be filled with as many flowers as will fit comfortably.

4   Place another piece of blotting paper on top of the page of flowers, and over this place one of the pieces of corrugated cardboard.

5   Repeat this procedure until you have a stack of six to ten layers.

6   Place the stack of sandwiched flowers on a solid surface and pile several heavy books on top of the pile.

This method is a good way to press a large quantity of flowers at one time. However, if you want to press just one page of flowers, lay the petals between two pieces of paper toweling and place it all between two pages of a thick book. Place the book on a table, then pile a few more books on top to weight it down.

Pressed flowers should be left for a minimum of one week, but it is better to wait even longer before using them. The blotting paper or toweling absorbs the moisture in the flowers as they dry out. Once the moisture is completely absorbed, the flowers will be brittle and should be handled carefully.

When using pressed flowers, it takes many more coats of sealer to render the object usable. When working on a tabletop, for example, this could mean as many as thirty to forty coats. Don't let this turn you off. Water-based sealers dry very quickly, and it takes only ten or fifteen minutes to apply each coat.

Pressed flowers dry to an almost transparent thinness and are extremely delicate. Handling these tissue-paper-thin petals takes finesse. Using tweezers makes it easy to lift and position them.

Apply a thin coating of polyurethane to the surface of the object. Then lay each petal on the wet surface and press down gently with a wet paintbrush. Continue to add designs in this way. Step back and assess your work as you go along. When the design is complete, let the flowers dry overnight.

All petals and leaves must be evenly coated with sealer, and it's especially important that each coat dry thoroughly before adding another. With each additional coat, the leaves and petals become embedded under the sealer until the surface is smooth to the touch. This sort of project takes patience, but the result can be quite special.

Mission Table

I find that designing on a painted background is always easier than working on a piece stained a wood color. Colorful cutouts, especially flowers, seem to look prettier against white or pastels. However, stained wooden furniture has a rich finish and can be quite an elegant background when you choose the right designs.

When preparing unfinished furniture pieces in the studio, we choose which ones will be painted and which will look best stained. This decision is based on the type of wood the furniture is made of as well as its shape and size and where we think it will be used. For example, hardwood looks better when stained because the stain brings out the pretty grain in hardwood and gives it character. Pine furniture looks best painted because there are often knots in the wood, which tend to get darker under the stain. Unfinished hardwood is better-quality wood than pine, so we usually treat the pine with a sealer to conceal the knots and then give it two or three coats of latex paint. It is harder for me to come up with a good design for the stained pieces, but I find the variety of stained and painted pieces in a room to be more interesting than everything matching. I also like a mix of different wood tones and colors of painted furniture used together.

We chose a maple stain for a hardwood mission-style table. After it was stained and ready for découpage, I walked by and around it for weeks. Every now and then I tried one of my paper cutouts in the center of the table. A sunflower was pretty but not large enough to create a dramatic design. I tried to create a border of flowers around the rim, but it looked ordinary. None of my cutouts seemed to go with the style of the table.

While searching through an atlas I use for pressing flowers, I found rose petals, poppy petals, and lots of leaves that I had pressed the previous year. Some of the petals had turned brown, but the poppies still had a faint lilac shade—and when I scattered this treasure trove of dried materials over the tabletop, I knew I had found the right look. The stain was visible through the translucent petals, making them blend with the background in a not-too-contrasty way.

A mission-style table is découpaged with dried poppy petals covered with many coats of sealer.

SPECIAL EFFECTS

A variety of faux finishes can be used to create an interesting textured background onto which you can apply découpage designs. I use the technique of antiquing over a finished piece to make it look old. When I am creating a nautical theme, for example, I often use the technique of sponging with blue paint to simulate water. Ragging and crackling are other popular techniques you might like to know about. Stippling is fun and can be used to create a colorful background on kitchen chairs or a floor, for example.

For many years I mixed glazes and paints in an effort to create all sorts of painted finishes such as sponging, ragging, and color washing. When I first started doing découpage, there was no such thing as water-based finishes, which now make the technique easier. New and improved products make it possible to focus more on the creative aspects of the craft.

Instead of throwing away an outdated vase or tired watering can, spray on a coat of any desired finish and it will be brand-new. We can create the look of stone, leather, or verdigris, to name just a few faux finishes.

Antiquing

I recently gave a talk and demonstration on the art of découpage in Florence, Italy. After applying all the coats of sealer, I "antiqued" the finish to give character to the box on which I was working. When I got to this step in my lecture, my audience of Italian men and women began to laugh. I asked what they found so funny, and one woman said, "Leslie, in Florence everything is old. We don't try to make things *look* old." Of course, in the United States we appreciate things that are worn and have stood the test of time, even if we have to help them along a bit.

This is an optional step but a technique that is quite effective when I want to make a piece look like an antique.

1   If you apply antiquing, *do not sand* the last coat of sealer. Sanding creates invisible scratches on the surface that become visible when the antiquing mixture is applied.

2   To give your piece the look of natural aging, mix a drop of water with a tablespoonful of water-based raw umber from a tube (available in art stores) and apply it with an artist's pointed brush. Dip your brush into the raw umber mixture and, working on one small area at a time, apply the "antiquing." Before it has time to dry, use a soft rag to lightly wipe away most of this dark coating, leaving traces around the cutouts and in the corners of a box, for example, to simulate wear and tear and to indicate where dirt may have ordinarily collected over time.

3   Continue to do this on the entire object, taking care to blend the antiquing between sections. If the piece looks too dirty, wet the rag slightly and wipe away more of the mixture, leaving a slight film on the surface.

4   Let the paint dry for one to two hours and then coat the entire piece with the sealer as before. Once the sealer is dry, sand the piece lightly with fine sandpaper.

Sponging

Sponging with a sea sponge is the easiest and quickest way to create a textured finish over a painted surface. It involves sponging a glaze-paint mixture over a flat painted surface.

1   Apply a base coat of a pale-color paint such as ivory or pastel blue with a regular paintbrush or roller.

2   Dampen and squeeze dry a sea sponge. (This is different from a kitchen sponge, as it is an irregular shape with crevices. You'll find it in an art or craft supply store.)

3   To apply the first glaze color, dip the sponge in the glaze (medium green, for example) and sponge it off on a newspaper to remove the excess glaze.

4   Sponge the surface in a random pattern. To avoid a uniform look, continually turn the sponge in different directions as you pat it onto the surface. Sponge, lift, turn, and sponge again.

5   Allow the glaze to dry before sponging on another color, if desired.

6   Gently sponge the second glaze (perhaps a blue color) over the entire surface, leaving open areas here and there.

7   Continue to sponge on color until the surface looks good to you.

8   When the second color is dry, go back and sponge more of the first color glaze, if you want to. The more subtle the pattern, the better it will look.

9   Continue to add more of whichever color you think is needed until you're satisfied.

Spattering

For a spatter paint treatment, you need the same items as used for sponge painting except you substitute a toothbrush for the natural sponge. Once the furniture is painted in the background color and completely dry, add spatters of color over all surfaces.

1   Put a small amount of the second paint color in a shallow dish. Dip the toothbrush into the color and wipe off the excess paint onto newspaper.

2   Then, while holding the brush over the painted item, run your thumb over the bristles so the paint spatters in a random pattern. Continue to cover the furniture with spatters of paint.

3   Continue as for sponge painting.

Crackling

Lately, crackle finish has become a popular background for découpage, but it can also be used by itself as an interesting way to refinish furniture. This is a glazed finish that looks as though the painted surface were cracked overall. The appearance is like that of a cracked eggshell. Crackle glaze was invented in France in the eighteenth century. It was inspired by the lacquer finish of imported Oriental ceramics and Japanese raku pottery. Today it is used by faux finishers to add faded character to a painted piece of furniture, moldings, picture and mirror frames, and small boxes. Since découpage and crackle finish are both French in origin, the combination could be described as "a little crafting with a French twist."

For small projects that require quick crafting, you'll find premixed solutions in most craft stores. However, to make the real thing, the process involves applying one interacting varnish over another. Art stores carry the materials needed, which include oil- and water-based varnishes, transparent oil glaze, raw umber oil paint in a small tube, and cheesecloth. This is an interesting finish and one you might enjoy trying. Practice on a scrap of wood before actually applying it to a large piece of furniture.

1   Start with a clean, lightly sanded object. Paint the piece in a color of your choice using latex, oil enamel, or acrylic paint.

2   Apply the *oil-based* varnish in a smooth, thin layer. Let the varnish dry until it is slightly tacky.

3   Brush on a coat of *water-based* varnish, covering the entire surface completely. Let it dry for about an hour. Cracks will appear.

4   To accentuate the cracks and give the piece an antiqued look, mix a small amount of raw umber with a tablespoonful of transparent oil glaze. Use the cheesecloth to rub the mixture all over the surface.

5   Rub away the excess without removing it from the cracks. Let it dry for several days. Then apply a coat of oil-based varnish if you want or simply wipe a damp sponge all over the piece, leaving traces of color in the cracks.

6   If you want to use a specific color, either paint the background in that color or use the color rather than raw umber to give the cracks a brighter look.

7   Once you have the crackle background, apply the cutouts for découpage and cover it with layers of sealer, as you would on a plain painted surface.

Ragging

The best faux finishers create amazing effects with this incredibly simple technique for achieving patterned surfaces. The textures can be hard-edged and strong or imperfect and subtle, depending on the colors you choose and the way you employ the technique. Choose your style. Imperfect is always my choice.

1   Scrunch up a rag, dip it in glaze, and press it onto a painted background. This is a trial-and-error technique. You have to press the rag with different amounts of pressure to see which results you like best.

2   Continually turn your rag to create a random pattern. Let some of the base coat show through for best results.

3   Stand back to check your work as you go along.

4   For a richer finish, wait until the first coat of glaze is dry and then rag on a second glaze color.

Glazing

Glaze is a combination of water-based paint, acrylic medium, and water. Acrylic medium is a milky white liquid that, when mixed with paint, makes a translucent mixture. Acrylic medium is available in art stores, craft stores, and home centers that carry decorative finishing materials. Craft and paint stores have faux finishing paints and glazes in decorator colors, but you can mix your own. Here's a recipe that offers a very basic formula.

1   Mix together one ounce of paint and one ounce of acrylic medium.

2   Add water to thin the mixture, two or three drops at a time, and mix thoroughly.

3   As you add water, try out the glaze. If it is too thick to apply easily, add more water, a drop at a time.

4   When applying glaze over a large painted area, do so in small sections at a time. Then the glaze doesn't have time to dry while you're working with it.

7 THE IMPORTANCE OF ACCESSORIES

A FEW YEARS AGO when I was a guest on *The Oprah Winfrey Show*, Oprah made a statement about decorating: "It's the accessories that I focus on." Indeed, while comfort and style are important furniture features, it's the accessories that give a home personality.

If you ask a handful of decorators what they consider a necessity, some will mention fabrics, others window treatments, and many will say a good antique piece for character. When you walk into a room that's well designed, usually the first thing you notice is the overall effect. When we adjust to the environment, we pick up on the details: color, furniture arrangement, lighting, and other subtle effects. But without the objects on the coffee table, the plants or flowers, the lamps, the mirrors and artwork on the walls, the room wouldn't seem as pleasing or well designed.

THIS PAGE

Découpage glass jars and bottles as accessories add charm to a bathroom, desk, or kitchen area. Be sure the neck is wide enough to insert a 1-inch-wide foam brush for applying the glue and the paint to the inside of the bottle.

OPPOSITE

A collection of wooden shoe lasts used by shoemakers to form shoes is displayed on an Early American folk art cabinet and a miniature chair. I especially like the ones made for children's shoes. I painted them and covered them completely with delicate flowers.

For that particular *Oprah* show I was asked to do two makeovers in my house. The first was a formal look, followed by a more casual country look. But when I went out to Chicago to do a live show, the producer wanted me to demonstrate making a few accessories that I thought the audience might use in their own homes. During my segment of the show I talked about handmade objects and showed how to make my reverse découpage plates. I also showed how to make a découpage floorcloth and showed a few examples of my handmade découpage boxes. Oprah commented on her own passion for handmade objects near and dear to her that made her home her very own.

Accessorizing a room is a personal matter. It doesn't have to cost an arm and a leg to accessorize with interesting and one-of-a-kind items. In fact, you can use the art of découpage to transform ordinary, everyday items into future heirlooms. Something as humble as a glass apothecary jar or tiny aspirin tins have just as much potential as an antique lamp base.

OPPOSITE

A Swedish breadbox has a lovely round shape, and I found the perfect print of a round pumpkin on the vine for it. When placed on a scrubbed pine sideboard, it is outstanding.

RIGHT

Enhance your front door with a number plaque. The design might be playful as shown on the no. 3 or it might be subdued like the no. 78 surrounded by leaves. You can also personalize a door plaque. A plaque on a southern home might be designed with magnolia blossoms. If you live on Goldfinch Drive, for example, you might incorporate that bird into your découpage.

OPPOSITE

I always use one of my Christmas plates in an arrangement with greens and candles during the holidays.

RIGHT

Tiny aspirin tins can be painted and decorated with the smallest of cutouts.

BELOW

Craft stores carry unfinished wooden boxes in different sizes and shapes for découpage projects. This simple box is painted soft green and découpaged with white flowers. It's a perfect desk accessory for holding paper clips.

8 WHAT NEXT?

I THOUGHT I HAD DÉCOUPAGED just about everything I could think of that would make sense to decorate this way. However, every creative person I know has that one project he or she has always dreamed of. It might be something he or she plans to do in the future, something that is germinating, or something he or she would like to do but may never get to.

In this regard, years ago I was invited to the studio of the artist Gloria Vanderbilt. She had written a book about her collages (one of my favorite books), and we had a lot in common, including that we both showed our work in galleries on Nantucket. I was greatly impressed with her studio in New York because she had découpaged the entire floor with cut-out prints and bits of memorabilia in the style of her paintings and collages. Ever since that wonderful experience, I have dreamed of doing such a project and have filed this idea away under "Projects I intend to do someday." I can still visualize that floor and have designed, in my mind, a similar project many times over. It just hasn't happened, but perhaps one day my studio floor will be as grand as Ms. Vanderbilt's. For now, however, it is spattered with paint and not a very pretty picture. Perhaps some things are better left to one's imagination than meant to become a reality.

ACKNOWLEDGMENTS

As an author of many books on crafts and decorating, I am most grateful to have been given the opportunity to present a lifetime of my work in a very personal way. Without the enthusiasm and support of Jill Cohen and Karen Murgolo at Bulfinch Press, this book couldn't have been produced as I had envisioned it. Their selection of Karyn Gerhard as my editor was another blessing. Karyn's sensitivity to the material was a writer's dream and working with her was a joyful experience. I also want to thank Joel Avirom and his team for their creative approach to designing the book. Most of all, I want to acknowledge my agent, Linda Konner, for being the consummate professional that she is. Her input and insight are what enabled this project to become a reality. Thanks also to my former agent, Alan Kellock, whose advice helped steer me to Linda. I extend extreme gratitude to my wonderful friends in Nantucket and Key West who provided me with outstanding environments in which to showcase my work: Peggy and Eli Kaufman, Nancy Norris, Walt and Josine Hitchcock, Carol and Gerry Fauth, Maryann and Jerry Gelula, Toby Greenburg, and Michael Sederback and Bob Arrick, who own Patina, where I found great stuff to découpage. Thank you, George Korn and Richard Kemble, for a dream house and studio in Key West in which to create the projects, write, photograph, and also squeeze in some much-needed vacation time. Thanks also go to our most capable friend, Jeff Allen, who helped us with much of the photography and who is always cheerful, even when I'm not. Most of all, I am grateful to have a partner who is the perfect complement to my talent and personality, my husband, Jon Aron. I could never do what I do without him.

Leslie Linsley

You can contact Leslie Linsley at Leslie@leslielinsley.com.